Moving to Canada

A complete guide to immigrating to Canada without an attorney

Cori Carl

Contents

Introduction

People talk about moving to Canada all the time, but there's little helpful information available detailing how to actually do it. That's what I discovered when I decided to make the move from Brooklyn, New York, to Toronto, Ontario. Now that I'm a permanent resident of Canada, I've written the guide I wish I'd had when I began.

Most of the ways you can legally move to Canada have the same process, regardless of your citizenship or where you're currently living. Many Americans and people from the Commonwealth are surprised to discover there's no fast track program for us.

Immigration, Refugees and Citizenship Canada (IRCC) has a very thorough website that's designed to enable people to apply for Canadian residency without the help of an immigration consultant or attorney. However, the website is still the product of a bureaucracy. Their instructions are meant to be applicable for anyone, coming from anywhere, under any circumstances. Most of the forums and other resources available are for people coming from non-Western cultures, who have very different concerns than I did. This book is written for people coming from countries that are culturally similar to Canada, like Britain and its former colonies.

Many existing third-party guides are outdated, since the IRCC made major changes in early 2015 and has continued to make adjustments each year. Other immigration guides are merely advertisements to scare you into hiring someone from the author's firm to serve as your attorney.

I'm not an attorney. This book is the product of obsessive research and real life experience. You should always consult the IRCC website or a professional before forging ahead. Making a mistake on a visa application is not something you want to deal with.

If you want professional legal advice, you should consult an immigration attorney or accredited immigration consultant. Hiring someone to do your application for you will not improve your odds of having it approved, nor will it speed up the process. They can simply make sure your application is complete and doesn't contain mistakes.

Many of us move to Canada each year without getting professional help with the application or moving process. I was able to navigate the process on my own and I'm sharing everything I've learned with you in this guide.

Part One: Canadian essentials

There are a lot of factors to consider before moving to Canada and a lot of different ways to make the move. Some people decide to move to Canada with an abundance of first-hand knowledge about what their life in Canada will be like, while others move to a city they've picked off a map or because of rumors of job prospects in a country they've never been to. I'll walk you through the basics you need to know about Canada so you can get an idea of what life in Canada is really like.

You want to move to Canada, eh?

Moving to another country is never as simple as packing your stuff and jumping on a plane. In order to legally live and work in another country, you'll have to go through the necessary government channels to make sure you're not breaking any international laws.

Luckily, Canada is eager for new residents from around the world. They've designed their visa and immigration programs to be simple. They may not seem simple, but that's only because you probably have nothing to compare them to. How many people immigrate to multiple countries? Not many.

To work legally in Canada, you'll need to be a Canadian citizen, permanent resident, or have a valid work visa. Depending on which country you're a citizen of, there's a good chance you can visit Canada for up to six months without needing to apply in advance for a visa. This won't allow you to accept a job, but it's a good opportunity to get to know the country and start building your professional network.

If you work in a field that requires licensing or certification, you'll want to find out whether or not your credentials will be recognized and what it will take to be re-licensed or re-certified in Canada.

There's no fast track to immigrate to Canada based on your nationality. This includes you, citizens of the United States and the United Kingdom. However, the working holiday program and NAFTA (yes, that's still around) do make it easier for people from some countries to live in Canada temporarily, which gives you an advantage if you decide to move to Canada permanently.

Things you should know about Canada

You're not alone in considering moving to Canada from abroad:

- Canada welcomes around a quarter of a million immigrants each year.
- Unlike most western nations, Canadians generally support their high per capita immigration rate.
- Support for immigration is increasing and all major Canadian political parties support it.
- 22% of Canadians are first-generation immigrants.
- Nearly half of people living in Toronto are foreign-born.
- Nearly half of all immigrants to Canada settle in the Greater Toronto Area.

- Because Canadian immigration is based primarily on a points system, immigrants to Canada are overall better educated and better paid than immigrants to the United States.
- Many of Canada's most highly educated (and highest paid) workers were born outside of Canada.

Let's cover the basics:
- Canada is a bilingual country. English and French are both official languages of Canada and receive equal status in the government
- The national capital is Ottawa, Ontario
- Canada has ten provinces and three territories, making thirteen co-sovereign jurisdictions
- Queen Elizabeth II is the Queen of Canada and thus Canada is a member of the Commonwealth of Nations
- Canada is a constitutional monarchy, a parliamentary democracy, and a federal state
- Toronto is the 4th largest city in North America
- Nearly one in three Canadians live in the country's three biggest cities: Toronto, Montreal, and Vancouver
- Québec is basically a different country
- The Québécois aren't the only French speaking Canadians; there are also the Acadians and other scattered Francophone communities
- Canada has a very complicated relationship with the Aboriginal peoples (First Nations, Inuit, and Métis) who originally settled the country and remain sovereign nations
- Newfoundland was a self-governing country until 1949
- Canada is the second largest country by area, covering 10 million square kilometres (or nearly 3.9 million square miles)

Sorry, you can't just become a citizen

If you aren't currently a citizen of Canada, you can't simply apply to become one.

Typically, first you apply to become a resident of Canada. Most people do this by going to university in Canada or getting a job that qualifies them for a work permit.

Sometimes being a Canadian resident can make you eligible to become a permanent resident (PR) of Canada. Permanent residents have almost all of the same rights as Canadian citizens. The main difference is that people with PR status can't vote and they must live in the country for a certain amount of time to maintain their residency.

In some cases, people can live as residents of Canada for a long time and never qualify to become a permanent resident.

Some immigration programs, like Express Entry, will allow people to become a permanent resident without requiring that they be a resident first.

After having lived in Canada as a permanent resident for several years, most people become eligible to apply for citizenship.

Some people choose to remain permanent residents because their country of origin doesn't allow dual citizenship and they don't want to renounce their original nationality. Other people may simply be happy as permanent residents and don't feel the need to go through the hassle and expense of applying for citizenship.

Immigration consultants & attorneys

If you're comfortable in English and good with managing paperwork, you'll likely have no problem completing the application to move to Canada on your own, without assistance from a lawyer or immigration consultant. If you're planning on moving to Quebec, replace "English" with "French" in that last sentence and it holds true.

You may want to get assistance with the process if you don't feel comfortable with your language skills, are worried about extenuating circumstances, or are intimidated by filling out government forms.

If you happen to ask an immigration consultant if their services are required, they're likely to imply that the process is so overwhelming that you'd be lost without their help, or maybe even lead you to believe that they can somehow speed up the process. Neither of those things is true.

Admissibility to Canada

If you're deemed inadmissible, you can't enter Canada, even as a tourist. It's a show stopper. If you're inadmissible and you'd still like to move forward with moving to Canada, then you will probably need to hire an immigration attorney.

Your criminal record

You may be deemed to be temporarily or permanently inadmissible to Canada based on prior arrests or convictions. Temporary inadmissibility is up to the discretion of the border patrol agent and varies depending on your personal history. Canada and the US share databases for some things, including arrest records. A friend of mine was turned away at the border because of an arrest and told he couldn't enter Canada until five years had passed from the date of the arrest.

Some things that may make you permanently inadmissible to Canada are: DUI/DWI, theft, assault, drug trafficking, or being convicted of a crime that carried a sentence of 10 years or more.

If you're criminally inadmissible, you can apply for individual rehabilitation to your local visa office.

Medical inadmissibility

Your residency application could be denied if you have a high potential to place an excessive demand on health or social services. This is the case if your needs are high enough that they could impact wait times in the region you plan to relocate to or if they exceed the excessive demand cost threshold. The 2019 threshold is $102,585 over 5 years (or $20,517 per year). This amount is updated each year.

The excessive demand cost threshold doesn't apply to refugees, protected persons, and family sponsorship of dependent children, spouses, or common-law partners. This policy was updated and clarified in 2018 due to public outcry.

You can also be deemed inadmissible if you're determined to be a risk to public health or safety. This would be the case if you have an infectious disease (like active TB or syphilis), are at risk of being incapacitated by a health condition (like dementia), or demonstrate unpredictable or violent behavior.

If you are deemed medically inadmissible, the IRCC will send you a procedural fairness letter which outlines their decision and reasoning. You can reply to this letter with evidence to dispute their decision. You can also provide a mitigation plan to show how you will manage the impact of your health on Canada's public services.

Your country of origin

Coming from the US or the Commonwealth

Many people assume that American and Commonwealth citizens get some special shortcut to move to Canada. A lot of people don't even realize that Americans or citizens of the Commonwealth need to do something besides showing up at the border with all their stuff. Officially, being a US or Commonwealth nation citizen doesn't give you any special privileges.

However, Canada wants new residents to be able to quickly adapt to their new home and succeed. Being from a culturally similar country dramatically increases the likelihood that you'll do well in Canada. If you're from one of these countries, you probably:
- Are fluent in English and/or French
- Have an education Canadian employers will recognize

- Have a similar office culture
- Have family in Canada, or at least know a few people
- Are used to a similar cost of living
- Have documents in English and/or French and thus don't need to be translated

While you don't get any points for being from the US, or even from the British Empire, you're more likely to meet the basic requirements, are saved the expense of translation, and face less uncertainty in regards to education credential assessments and language exams.

Moving to Canada from outside of the commonwealth

There's no reason to worry if you're coming from a country that isn't the US, isn't part of the Commonwealth, or doesn't keep official documents in English or French. You're still going to follow the same process and meet the same requirements.

If you're concerned about your education being recognized, there's a free tool to see what your foreign degree will be equivalent to. This is provided by a company called World Education Services (WES), one of the IRCC approved education assessment companies.

Getting your documents translated will add time and expense to your application process. You can't just use a friend who speaks French or do it yourself, you'll need an approved translator recognized by the IRCC.

Statuses and rights in Canada

Everyone in Canada is protected by the Canadian Charter of Rights and Freedoms. Your rights as a visitor, student, temporary worker, or resident in Canada are the same, regardless of your nationality.

Visitors

Visitors to Canada can open bank accounts, buy a home, or enroll in courses lasting less than six months without requiring any special status.

Depending on your nationality, you may require a visa. Your nationality may also determine how long that visa is for. Visitors from many countries, including the US, Australia, UK, and the UK don't have to apply for a visa to visit Canada, as they are automatically granted one at the border.

If you're not from the US, you'll need an electronic Travel Authorization (eTA), which you can apply for online and only takes a few minutes. When you get to the border, you may also have to:

- Provide detailed information about the reason for your trip and your plans
- Undergo a search
- Prove that you're the guardian of any kids with you
- Prove you have enough money for your trip
- Prove you have plans to return home
- Demonstrate ties to your home country

As a visitor, you can bring your own personal baggage and vehicles into Canada, but you may owe taxes on anything you leave in Canada. If you declare goods when you arrive and take them with you when you leave, you won't owe duty, but may be required to leave a security deposit for items with a high resale value.

You can be turned away at the border for any number of reasons. You need to be in good health, have proper travel documents, and convince the immigration officer that you will leave Canada when you are legally obligated to. You can also be determined to be criminally inadmissible to Canada if you have been convicted of a crime.

One tricky concept is dual intent. You may be visiting Canada while waiting for your immigration paperwork to go through or intending to get married to a Canadian on your trip. Dual intent is any situation where your intentions for your trip to Canada are unclear.

Dual intent can be reason to turn you away at the border. However, this is rarely the case. If you fall into multiple statuses or have a pending application for residency, be upfront about this with the border agent. Be ready to demonstrate that you understand immigration procedures, intend to follow them, and are really returning to your home country if your application is delayed or denied.

I entered Canada as a visitor several times after my Express Entry profile was submitted and even after my landing documents were issued. This attracted extra scrutiny at the border, but never caused anything more than a few minutes of delay. Be prepared to explain your situation and have any relevant documents on hand when traveling.

Temporary workers in Canada

There are two types of work permits that would allow you to reside in Canada as a temporary worker:

- Open work permits allow you to work for any employer in Canada except those deemed to be ineligible to hire foreign workers by the government.
- Employer specific work permits allow you to be employed by a specific company for a set amount of time, and sometimes in a specific location. You are permitted to look for a new job, but you will have to apply for a new work permit if you want to switch jobs.

Temporary workers in Canada are protected by Canadian laws and must pay Canadian taxes.

If you're granted a work permit, you can usually bring your spouse and children with you to Canada. However, they cannot work without getting their own work permit. A working holiday visa does not allow you to bring your partner or children.

As a temporary worker, you will need private health insurance until you become eligible for provincial health insurance. They may ask to see proof of your insurance coverage at the port of entry. If you have family members coming with you, they'll also need health insurance.

Temporary workers have the right to a safe and equitable workplace. Your employer:
- Cannot hold your passport or work permit
- Must compensate you for all work, including overtime
- Must allow for breaks and days off
- Cannot threaten your legal status in Canada
- Cannot force you to perform tasks that you were not hired for

Each province has its own worker protection laws, so they vary depending on where you're living in Canada.

Canadian permanent residents

You may be able to move to Canada as a permanent resident, like I did, or you may become eligible to become a permanent resident after living in Canada. With PR status, you:
- Can live, work, or study in Canada
- Are able to get most of the same benefits as citizens
- Must pay taxes and follow all laws at the federal, provincial, and municipal levels
- Can't vote or run for public office
- Can join the Canadian armed forces
- Can't hold certain jobs that require high-level security clearance
- May be deported if convicted of a serious criminal offense

Healthcare in Canada is managed at the provincial level, so while you're eligible for government health insurance, you may need to meet other requirements, such as living in that province for a certain amount of time.

As a permanent resident, you're expected to live in Canada for two out of every five years, on a rolling basis. If you're living outside of the country for more than three years, you can lose your PR status and be barred from returning to Canada until you apply for a new visa.

You'll need to carry your passport and your PR card when traveling outside the country. Allowing the card to expire doesn't mean you've lost PR status. If you've let your PR card expire while you're outside of the country, you'll need to get travel documents from the local visa office before you can return to Canada. This guarantees that they will check to make sure you've met your residency requirements (and is a preventable hassle).

If you were granted PR status in Canada and did not meet residency requirements, you don't automatically lose your PR status. In order to re-enter Canada, you will need to either talk your way into new travel documents or renounce your PR status and enter as a visitor.

Canadian citizens

After you've been physically present in Canada for 1,095 days (three years), you're eligible to apply for citizenship. The days do not have to be consecutive, but they need to be within five years.

If you've stayed in Canada for three years since you obtained PR status, determining when you're eligible to apply for citizenship is simple.

If you've traveled outside the country, you'll need to calculate the days using a tool provided by the IRCC. Time spent as a temporary resident (student, temporary worker, etc) can add up to a year to your residency requirements. Time spent in prison does not count. Even if you don't plan on applying for citizenship yet, you'll need to use the physical presence calculator to demonstrate that you've met your residency requirements to renew your PR card.

Your application will need to include proof that you can speak English or French and that you've paid your taxes. You'll also have to take a citizenship test, covering aspects of Canadian history, government, and culture.

Some government employees (and their families) can be fast tracked to citizenship.

If your original nationality allows dual citizenship, you do not have to renounce your citizenship in order to become a Canadian citizen. As a US, UK, or Australian citizen, you can be a dual citizen.

Canadian citizens have the right to
- Live, work, or go to school in Canada
- Vote in federal, provincial, territorial, or local elections, unless they've been living outside of Canada for more than five years
- Express yourself, gather peacefully and groups, and practice your religion freely
- Enter, remain in, or leave the country
- Be treated with the same respect, dignity, and consideration regardless of personal characteristics
- Have information presented, participate in government, and receive services in either English or French

Canadian citizens can
- Join the armed forces
- Benefit from social welfare programs, such as healthcare, which may have residency requirements
- Eliminate discrimination and injustice, help others in the community, and protect our heritage and environment

Canadian citizens have the duty to
- Respect the rights and freedoms of others
- Obey Canada's laws and pay taxes
- Participate in the democratic process by serving on a jury
- Respect Canada's official languages and multicultural heritage
- New Canadian citizens get the Cultural Access Pass, allowing you to visit cultural institutions for free during their first year of citizenship.

If you are a dual citizen of Canada and another country, you will need a Canadian passport in order to return to Canada if your other nationality requires an eTA to enter Canada. Canadian citizens cannot be given an eTA, therefore they require a Canadian passport. As of 2019, US citizens do not require an eTA when traveling internationally.

Canada's best cities for newcomers

Canada is a huge country with an incredible diversity in terms of city size, weather, and geography. There's surely somewhere that will be the right fit for you.

Best weather

- **Kelowna, BC** has hot summers and rarely drops below freezing in winter. It's also rarely windy.
- **Osoyoos, BC** stays warm year round and is rarely humid. Centered on a lake, this is a great spot for outdoor enthusiasts.
- **Victoria, BC** is known for its beauty, tourist-friendly amenities, and warm weather. It gets more sun than Seattle and very little snow (if any). You can easily reach Vancouver, Seattle, Portland, and amazing hiking.
- **Niagara-on-the-Lake, ON** is in Canada's wine region, with easy access to hikes along the Niagara escarpment. The winters are similar to upstate New York. It provides easy to access to jobs and attractions in Toronto, Hamilton, Buffalo, and even Detroit.
- **Banff, AL** might seem like a surprising choice, unless you like to ski and hike.

Best job prospects

The best place to find a job is the city you have the most professional connections in. Some cities are hubs for specific industries. Kitchener-Waterloo and Guelph are home to many tech companies and startups. Ottawa is the place to be for government jobs. Calgary is home to much of the oil and gas industry. Toronto is the leader for banking and insurance.

Generally speaking, these cities have the most available jobs.

- Toronto, ON
- Kitchener-Waterloo, ON
- Vancouver, BC
- Abbotsford, BC
- Saskatoon, SK
- Edmonton, AB

Best cities for bilingual immigrants

New Brunswick is Canada's only bilingual province. In Quebec, much of the signage is only in French and people in small towns may not speak any English at all.

- Ottawa, ON & Gatineau, QC
- Montreal, QC
- Quebec City, QC
- Fredericton, NB
- Saint John, NB
- Moncton, NB

Easiest to get provincial nomination
Bilingual English & French: Ontario
Canadian Graduate: Ontario
Farmers: Saskatchewan & Manitoba
Investors: Yukon & Northwest Territories

If you're currently living in Canada as a student or worker, your province probably has a program to enable you to become a permanent resident.

Climate

Canada is not a frigid polar land, contrary to popular misconceptions. Canada is a huge country with several climate zones. Most of the population is within 100 miles of the US border, so the climate is very similar on both sides.

I've found Toronto to be a few degrees cooler than New York City, so the summers aren't as brutal and the winters are a little rougher. Only in Toronto they have underground walkways and are prepared for anything, whereas, my neighborhood in Brooklyn never got shoveled and the subway would be shut down without notice. This is very New York specific, but it was incredibly exciting to move to Toronto and have a modern heating system that I could control myself. While the winters in Toronto might technically be colder, my everyday experience of getting around the city is far more pleasant.

Montreal and Ottawa are both significantly colder than Toronto and get more snow. However, this doesn't keep people indoors. Montreal is full of street festivals featuring fires and mulled wine that run late into the evening. In Ottawa the canal system turns into a giant ice skating rink and people go skiing (cross-country or across the border in Quebec) every free afternoon.

Economy

Canada is one of the world's wealthiest nations, with a high standard of living and frequently ranks among the top places to live in terms of quality of life. It has a high level of economic freedom, ranking 9th in the 2018 index. It's the most free economy in the Americas and the tenth largest economy in the world. The Toronto Stock Exchange (TSX) is the third largest stock exchange in North America, after the NYSE and Nasdaq.

Three quarters of the population works in the service industry. These include trades, healthcare, finance, education, food, retail, and government. Manufacturing is largely centered in Ontario and Quebec. Central Canada still has a farming economy, growing wheat, corn, oilseed, cattle, and pigs. The country is currently moving forward with significant infrastructure upgrades.

In addition to the second largest oil reserves in the world, Canada's natural resources include natural gas, gold, nickel, aluminum, fish, and timber. Canada has more freshwater than any other country. Canada has trade agreements with the US and Mexico (NAFTA, soon to be replaced by USMCA), the EU (CETA), the Caribbean (CARICOM), non-EU countries, India, Japan, and much of South America. They're a member of the WTO and have signed the TPP.

Canada's economy is closely linked to that of the US, as the US is Canada's top export and import partner. Some economists treat both countries as a single economic entity. Half of all foreign investments in Canada come from the US. Canada is America's largest source of fuel imports.

Climate change could boost the Canadian economy. The declining ice shelves could open the northern sea route and northwest passage to commercial traffic. It could also increase the amount of land usable for agriculture and lengthen the growing season. There is strong support for green environmental policies.

Taxes in Canada are lower than that of countries with a similar standard of living, like Germany, France, and Denmark. People are taxed progressively based on their income. Canada has one of the lowest rates of corporate taxes in the world.

Quality of life compared to the US

Canadian cities frequently place at or near the top of quality of life rankings.

- Canadians have a high level of life satisfaction compared to Americans
- Canadians get more paid time off
- Parents get 50 weeks of paid leave to welcome new children
- Canadians work fewer hours
- Net worths are higher
- Fewer marriages break up
- The infant mortality rate is lower and the life expectancy is longer

If you're a visible minority, your odds are better in Canada. Canada hasn't overcome discrimination, but Canada is an easier place to live than the US. There are fewer incidences of bias and they're less extreme. Income disparity is a problem in Canada, but a much smaller problem compared to the US.

Canada is much safer than the US. Non-violent crime rates are roughly similar, but violent crimes are much, much lower in Canada.

Canadians who live in Vancouver, Toronto, or Montreal will complain endlessly about how expensive it is. Coming from New York City, I find this hilarious. Canadian cities are significantly less expensive than their American counterparts. The best example is real estate, which seems very expensive in Canadian cities, unless you've ever looked at renting or buying in New York or San Francisco...or Tokyo.

If you're not coming from a major city, you may find the cost of living to be higher in Canada. The price of goods in Canada reflects the actual cost of the items, whereas, in the US, the government covers the cost of corporate pollution and allows wages too low for many workers to live off of.

Economy

The Canadian dollar and the US dollar are not the same, although they often have a similar value. Most of the goods flowing in and out of Canada are through trade with the United States. China is Canada's second biggest trading partner.

The Canadian banking system is one of the most stable in the world. Canada's economy fared better than the US during the most recent recession, in part because Canada didn't have the subprime mortgage implosion.

Unions seem to be much more prevalent in Canada than in the US.

Government

Canada is regularly ranked as the most democratic nation in the Americas. It is a constitutional monarchy with a federal parliamentary democracy, in contrast to the federal constitutional republic of the US.

The Canadian Crown heads the executive, legislative, and judicial branches of government. The head of state has been Queen Elizabeth II since 1952. Canadian laws are based on English Common Law, except in Québec.

Taxes for US citizens and green card holders

It's hard to compare tax rates between the US and Canada because there are so many variables. Overall, the actual amount of money you pay in taxes is comparable between the US and Canada. However, taxes in Canada include nearly all healthcare costs whereas in the US you pay your taxes, pay for health insurance, and then pay much higher out of pocket costs.

The US taxes your worldwide income, it's true. Being a successful American expat comes at a cost. While living abroad, you aren't taxed in the US on the first $104k USD of foreign earned income. If you're married and both living abroad, you can exclude your first $208k USD of income. Any income above that amount can be sheltered from taxes by depositing it into a retirement account, up to the limit.

If someone is complaining about double taxation, they either make a lot of money or they need a new accountant.

The US gives you credit for any taxes you pay in Canada. You also get tax breaks for things like housing costs. The US has agreements with Canada so you're covered under Social Security in whatever country you end up in, with credit for your employment in both countries.

For detailed information on taxes for US citizens and greencard holders living in Canada, see Cross Border Taxes: A complete guide to filing taxes as an American in Canada.

Healthcare

Canada has a publicly funded single payer healthcare system, with private organizations providing services and the government health insurance covering most costs. The government doesn't provide any care directly and all patient information remains confidential. If you're from a country with universal healthcare, this all seems normal. If you're from the US, it's magic.

Imagine never having to fill out—or dispute—insurance claims again. Changing jobs or being unemployed has no impact on your health insurance coverage. You don't have to switch doctors when your plan changes or call around trying to find doctors who accept your plan. There are no lifetime limits or clauses about pre-existing conditions. You won't get hit by unexpected bills for pre-approved surgeries because someone who treated you while you were unconscious was out of network. There are no surprise facility fees that vary for no rhyme or reason.

There are no deductibles on basic healthcare and co-pays are very low compared to what most people pay in the US. Each province runs its own system and they may have residency requirements for enrollment.

In Ontario, you have to be living in the province as a legal resident for three months before you are eligible for government funded health insurance through the Ontario Health Insurance Plan (OHIP).

Patients choose their general practitioner (GP) and the GP makes referrals to specialists as needed. Preventive care is encouraged.

As you may have heard, there can be waiting lists for treatments that aren't urgent, although these seem comparable to similar services in the US, depending on your insurance coverage and ability to pay. To put this into perspective, remember that Canadians have a longer life expectancy than Americans.

If you encounter a rare disease and a proven treatment is only available in another country, the government will pay for you to fly there and get the care you need.

People unhappy with provincial coverage can opt to receive care from anywhere in the world so long as they're willing and able to pay out-of-pocket for those services. You'll occasionally see news coverage of people whose care was denied because Canadian doctors deemed treatment to be not medically necessary or because the patient is demanding a treatment that is unproven and anticipated to be unsafe or ineffective.

The Canadian health insurance system doesn't cover everything. Mental health care is covered in some circumstances. Coverage varies from province to province. You're on your own for prescription drugs, home care, long-term care, vision, and dental. Most employers cover these with supplemental insurance plans. Only about 15% of healthcare costs are paid out-of-pocket in Canada.

Prescription drug prices are negotiated by the provincial governments to keep costs down, leading to many Americans buying their medications from Canadian pharmacies.

People in Canada simply don't die of curable diseases. The *survivorship* rate for serious diseases like cancer are much higher in the US than in countries with public healthcare systems, but the *mortality* rates are the same. That suggests people in the US are being diagnosed and treated for conditions that could have been safely left untreated. Surgeries and medications can have serious, irreversible side effects, so over-treatment has serious negative impacts on quality of life. And, in the US, over-treatment can lead to bankruptcy. Healthcare costs are the leading cause of bankruptcy in the US.

Canada has no restrictions on abortion. Medical and recreational marijuana is legal.

Education

Education is provided at no cost through high school. School systems are managed by the provinces. Schooling is offered in both English and French. Canadian 15-year-olds score above Americans on standardized tests.

The thing that stands out to me as an American is that there are publicly funded religious schools in Ontario, Saskatchewan, and Alberta. This is because separate schooling was guaranteed in 1867 and it's never gone away.

More than half of Canadians have a college degree, a rate far higher than any other country.

Canadian colleges and universities may not be as internationally known as big name US schools, but all Canadian universities provide a high-quality academic experience, while the US struggles with diploma mills and predatory for-profit colleges. Canadian schools generally have much lower tuition rates, sometimes half as much as you're likely to find in America, even when students are paying international rates.

Part Two:
The Options

After 10 years in New York City, I decided I wanted to move to Toronto. At first glance, my prospects didn't look so great:

- I wasn't secretly a dual citizen
- I was married to an American
- I didn't have any relatives in Canada
- I didn't have a job offer from a Canadian company
- I didn't have a job offer that qualified for a visa through NAFTA
- I wanted to follow international laws

Luckily, Canada is eager for new residents and they make it easy for people to move there. In fact, one of the most confusing things about moving up to Canada is the number of options.

Before you read any further, there are a couple reasons why you wouldn't be able to apply for any of these programs. These include any situation where:

- you are a security risk,
- you have committed human or international rights violations,
- you have been convicted of a crime, or you have committed an act outside Canada that would be a crime,
- you have ties to organized crime,
- you have a serious health problem,
- you have a serious financial problem,
- you've previously been deported from any country, or
- one of your family members is not allowed into Canada

If you have a conviction, not all hope is lost. If the conviction is from before you turned 18, you're likely still eligible for immigration. If you can get a record suspension or discharge, or convince them you've been rehabilitated, you might be fine.

You will face significant immigration hurdles if you have been convicted of driving while drunk or on drugs.

If any of the above is relevant to you, you will want to hire an immigration attorney to decide if moving to Canada is really an option and to help you with your application.

One more important detail: Québec is different. In all things. They have their own work and immigration requirements that are different from the rest of Canada. I'll get into Québec-specific immigration later.

Pathways to Canadian Citizenship

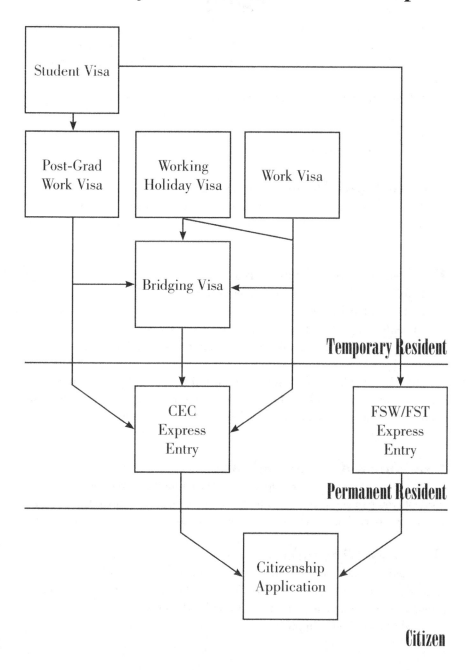

All the ways to live in Canada, legally

There are a lot of different ways to move to Canada. I'm going to explain all of the options briefly so you can decide which ones might be right for you. Once you've narrowed it down, you can learn more about each one later in the book.

While none of these programs take your nationality into consideration, there are certain perks to being from a culturally similar country. Many of the ways you can move to Canada are designed to be temporary, but provide a way to extend your stay permanently.

Live in Canada as an expat

There are a number of ways you can live in Canada legally on a temporary basis. These programs allow you to live in Canada a few months to a few years.

Take an extended vacation

If you don't plan on working while in Canada, you can stay in Canada as a tourist. Most tourist visas are issued for six months. At the end of your time, you can either apply to extend your tourist visa or simply leave the country and come right back. Doing this too often might raise some red flags at the border.

Visiting Canada can help you decide if you really want to move and where in Canada you'd like to live. It also gives you the opportunity to look for a job, check out schools, and look for love. Just remember, marrying someone for residency is a bad idea.

Visit your kids or grandkids

If you're the parent or grandparent of a Canadian citizen or permanent resident, you can get a super visa that allows you to stay for up to two years at a time for a period of ten years or they can sponsor you to become a resident.

Have a working holiday

Canada has agreements with a number of countries that allow young professionals under the age of 30 or 35 to work for up to two years in Canada through the International Experience Canada (IEC) program. After a year, you might be eligible to apply for permanent resident status.

Go (back) to school

Getting a university degree in Canada isn't the only way to get a student visa. You can also qualify by enrolling in a career training center, vocational school, or language school. As a student, you can work part-time during your studies. After you complete your program you can get a work permit for up to three years. You'll likely be eligible to apply to become a permanent resident before your work permit expires.

If you have a spouse or common law partner, they can work full-time during your studies. Depending on their job, you could both become permanent residents based on their work experience before you graduate.

Engage in free trade

Thanks to the North American Free Trade Agreement (NAFTA) and soon the United States-Mexico-Canada Agreement (USMCA), Canadian employers can easily hire American and Mexican citizens through a work permit. You can also work in Canada for up to six months without a work permit as a business visitor, trader, or investor.

Professionals can file for a TN work permit online and be issued a visa for up to three years within days. This is a streamlined process specifically for NAFTA/USMCA. You can apply for a new visa every three years with no limit on the number of times you get a TN visa.

If your company has an office in Canada they can transfer you up with little hassle.

Find a job

Depending on your career and your professional network, you may find it easy to get a job in Canada or you may find it impossible. In order to hire you, a company will have to get you a work permit, which requires that they show there's no Canadian worker available to take the job.

Become a migrant laborer

The Seasonal Agricultural Worker Program (SAWP) is one of the few programs that's different depending on your citizenship. If you're interested in this program, you'll need to go through your government directly.

Moving to Canada permanently

Most of the programs that allow people to become permanent residents of Canada require you to demonstrate that you have enough money to support yourself and your family while you get settled. Usually, this requirement is waived if you have a Canadian job offer. This amount starts at C$12.5k and increases along with the size of your family.

It doesn't matter if your family is moving to Canada with you or not, since you're still expected to support them. If you're in a relationship, your partner's savings counts toward the requirement. If you don't have a job lined up when you arrive or some sort of income, you'll burn through that money pretty quickly.

One of the (few) perks of applying for the Quebec Skilled Worker Program is that the proof of settlement funds starts at the considerably smaller C$3k.

If you don't have enough money in the bank, you'll need to apply as a refugee, be sponsored by a family member who can support you, or apply with a valid job offer.

You don't need to be legally married to your partner in order to bring them to Canada. Canada recognizes common law and conjugal partnerships.

If you immigrate to Canada, they won't make you leave your kids behind. Anyone under the age of 22 who's not married is considered a dependent that is eligible to come with you, as is anyone who relies on you because of a physical or mental condition.

Get serious with your Canadian girlfriend

Are you married to or in a serious relationship with a Canadian citizen or permanent resident? They can sponsor you to become a permanent resident. If you apply from inside of Canada, you can get a work permit while you wait for your application to be approved.

Use your family connections

If you have a relative in Canada who's willing to sponsor you, you might be able to become a permanent resident. There are a lot of restrictions on this program, so it's only the best option if it's the only option.

Be a business person

Running a startup? Canada is looking to hold its own against Silicon Valley, so they're building an excellent network to nurture startups and attract top talent. Up to five people can move to Canada under each startup visa. You'll need support from a designated VC fund, angel investor, or business incubator.

If you're an established entrepreneur or aspire to be one, most provinces have a Provincial Nominee Program (PNP) to help you move your business to Canada, start a new business in Canada, or buy an existing business.

Be awesome and self-employed

The self-employment immigration program is one of those great examples about how bureaucracy lumps weird things together sometimes. There are three categories of self-employed people who qualify for this program:

- World-class authors, writers, actors, musicians, etc.,
- World-class athletes, and
- Farmers

If you're a celebrity and you want to move to Canada, this is for you. You don't have to be a household name to qualify, since Canada is well aware that experts in certain fields are under-appreciated.

The federal program will soon be accepting farming applications through a new pilot program. PNPs are also accepting applications for experienced farmers.

Have skills they want

Express Entry is Canada's skilled worker program. If you're invited to apply as a skilled worker, you can become a permanent resident in about six months, even without a job offer.

You don't need to have advanced degrees or highly specialized skills to qualify. You might be surprised by the types of experience that are in demand. This program uses a points system, based on your age, language skills, education, work experience, connections to Canada, and adaptability.

Search the National Occupation Classification system to see if your job is listed in the 0, A, or B category.

- Skill Level 0: Management – almost any type of job that includes manager or supervisor in the title will qualify
- Skill Level A: Professional – most office jobs will qualify. Often these types of jobs will require some sort of degree, but that's not necessarily a requirement
- Skill Level B: Technical – these jobs often require an Associate's degree or apprenticeship of some kind.
- Skill Level C: Intermediate – high school diploma and/or on the job training is usually needed
- Skill Level D: Labor – typically have no education requirements and provide some sort of on the job training

The IRCC has a quiz to tell you if you qualify for Express Entry. It's a great tool to decide if it's worth it to start the process. Getting the paperwork will take some time and all the fees to get official copies, tests, and evaluations add up.

There are three immigration programs for skilled workers: Federal Skilled Workers, Canadian Experience Class, and Federal Skilled Trades Class.

Speak French

If you speak French fluently, you can get a temporary work permit through the Francophone Mobility program. It also makes you more likely to be selected for the various skilled worker programs.

Use your community

There are programs in some provinces for people with strong personal connections to someone in the province, such as a family member or close friend. You can also get a community group to sponsor you, such as if you are part of a faith or subculture with a tight-knit community in Canada.

These programs change regularly to meet the needs of the provinces and the application requires the complicated step of finding someone who is willing and eligible to sponsor you. Each province and each program has their own requirements and procedures.

These programs include:
- Manitoba Community Support
- Manitoba Family Support
- Nova Scotia Family Business Worker
- Prince Edward Islands Immigrant Connections
- Saskatchewan Family Members Category

Work as a caregiver

The caregiver programs that are open now are pilot programs, meaning they may not be renewed when they end in five years.

These pilot programs only accept people who will meet the requirements for permanent resident status once they have two years of work experience through the pilot program. Once you've completed your two years, there will be a pathway to PR status and then citizenship.

Spouses or common-law partners of participants in these pilots will receive open work permits and dependent children will be able to accompany their parents.

If you don't qualify for any of these pilot programs, you can get a regular temporary work permit if you have a job offer as a caregiver. However, your employer will need to get a LMIA and your work permit will only be valid for that employer.

Home Child Care Provider Pilot & Home Support Worker Pilot

In order to apply for either of these pilots, you need a job offer. However, your employer does not need to obtain a LMIA and you will be granted an occupation-specific open work permit. This means you are not forced to stay with the employer who originally offers you a job but you can't switch careers.

The application process is different depending on the experience you have as a professional caregiver and if you have worked as a caregiver in Canada before.

Each of these programs is limited to 2,750 principal applicants per year.

Closed caregiver pilot programs

The Live-in Caregiver Program (LCP) was a pilot program and is not open to new applicants. The backlog is almost finished being processed. Caregivers who misunderstood the temporary nature of previous caregiving pilots and would like to stay in Canada could apply for the Interim Pathway for Caregivers, which was originally scheduled to close in June 2019, but now closes October 2019.

The Caring for Children and Caring for People with High Medical Needs programs are also closed to new applicants.

Become a farmer

Starting in 2020, 2,750 principal applicants will be allowed to apply for PR status as farmers through a new three-year pilot program, announced in July 2019. Before you get too excited, this program requires that you already have experience in Canada's agri-food sector.

Eligible candidates will have at least 12 months of full-time, non-seasonal work under the Temporary Foreign Worker Program:

- meat processing (retail butcher, industrial butcher, or food processing labourer)
- harvesting labourer for year-round mushroom production and greenhouse crop production
- general farm worker for year-round mushroom production, greenhouse crop production, or livestock raising
- farm supervisor and specialized livestock worker for meat processing, year-round mushroom production, greenhouse crop production or livestock raising

The program also requires a CLB level 4 in English or French, a secondary school diploma, and a qualifying job offer for full-time, non-seasonal work in Canada, outside of Quebec, at or above the prevailing wage.

Details on how to apply for the Agri-Food Immigration Pilot will be available in early 2020.

Other provincial nomination programs

If you don't qualify for Express Entry, you may still be able to become a permanent resident through the Provincial Nomination Programs (PNP). These allow provinces and territories to select candidates based on their needs.

These programs change often, but most provinces have programs designed to retain people with connections to the province, especially people who are currently living, studying, or working there. Some communities with severe worker shortages even have their own programs within the PNP system.

Become a refugee

Regardless of the criticisms you may have of your home country, the refugee and asylum system almost certainly doesn't apply to you.

Programs that are no longer open

You used to be able to essentially buy your way into PR status by investing in Canadian businesses through several PNPs. This is no longer the case.

Retiring to Canada

There are no programs designed specifically to allow people to move to Canada for their retirement. Canada is already facing a large number of baby boomers retiring – as well as the ongoing care of the silent generation. Most immigration programs are designed to bring young professionals to Canada.

However, you may still be able to qualify to move to Canada, especially if you're excited about embarking on a second career while in Canada.

Long stays in Canada

If you're looking to spend your summers in beautiful Cape Breton, you're in luck. Visitors can spend up to six months a year in Canada without doing anything special. There's nothing stopping you from buying a vacation home on Prince Edward Island or in Prince Edward County. Theoretically you can stay for six months, leave the country for a day, and come right back for another six months. I imagine you'd face some extra questions at the border, though.

If you'd like to stay for more than six months, the easiest option is to extend your tourist visa. You need to do this at least 30 days before your current visitor visa expires. You have implied status while your application is processed, meaning your visa is considered to remain valid while the new application goes through. If you dream of spending a year exploring Canada before moving back home (or on to your next adventure) this is your best option. As a visitor, you'll need to have your own health insurance coverage and, depending on how long you stay, you may need to file taxes in Canada.

The parent and grandparent super visa will allow you to live in Canada for up to two years at a time, assuming you have kids or grandkids living in Canada.

Going back to school is another great temporary option. Have you always dreamed of studying your passion, getting your PhD, or becoming fluent in French? Doing so will provide you (and your partner) with residency for the duration of your program. You can even apply for a post-graduation work permit after your studies are complete, adding up to three years to your time in Canada.

Moving to Canada permanently

If you have children or grandchildren in Canada, they can sponsor you for permanent resident status through the family class program. If you don't have family to sponsor you, all other options require you to continue to work in Canada.

Many people dream of starting a business once they've become financially independent. Canada has various entrepreneur and investor programs that you may qualify for.

Express Entry for established professionals

Canada's skilled worker program, Express Entry, is designed to bring young professionals into the country. While it's relatively easy to qualify if you're under 35, it's still possible to qualify into your 40s if you have previous Canadian work experience, speak French, have advanced degrees, and especially if you have a qualifying job offer.

Express Entry awards points for your age. Someone in their 20s gets 100 points. Someone over 45 gets zero. However, you can still get enough points without those 100 points – you only need around 450 points (or less) out of a total of 1200 points. A PhD gets you 140 points.

Use your Canadian ties

You're not living in Canada now, but if you've lived in Canada at any point in your life, this can help you accumulate enough points to qualify for Express Entry.

If your degree is from Canada, you'll be awarded more points than if your degree is from any other country. You can get up to 30 points.

Have you ever worked in Canada? Five years of Canadian work experience gets you 80 points.

If you have a sibling living in Canada who's a citizen or permanent resident, you'll get 15 additional points.

Leverage your expertise to get a job

Getting a job offer can easily get you an invitation to apply. If you're an experienced professional who can use your network to land a job, this is a great way to get permanent resident status.

A qualifying job offer in skill level 0, A, or B will get you 50 points.

A job offer in high level management will get you 200 points.

If none of these options is right for you, there are plenty of other places that are eager to welcome retirees.

Part Three: Move to Canada as an Expat

Not every international move has to be a permanent one. Many people want to live in Canada for a few years before returning home or moving on to their next destination. In popular tourist destinations and major cities it can seem like everyone you meet is there on a working holiday visa. Canadian universities are full of international students. Canadian offices thrive thanks to international workers spicing up their CVs to make them more marketable back home.

Perhaps you are interested in potentially staying forever, but you want to make sure it's the right choice for you before you commit. Maybe you don't qualify to become a permanent resident right away, but you'd like to become one. I'll go over how each of these options sets you up to become a citizen.

Life as a perpetual tourist

If you can get a tourist visa to enter Canada, you can generally stay for six months. Many countries, like the US, UK, and Australia, don't require you to do anything to get a tourist visa. The length of your visa is at the discretion of the border agent, but it's rare for them to not give you six months automatically.

This is the simplest solution if you'd like to have a vacation home in Canada, but don't really want to uproot your life and move. I went back and forth between Toronto and New York for almost two years and had no problem. Occasionally I'd get a few extra questions at the border, but it never took more than a few minutes because I had a home in both cities, a job in New York, and always had a return flight booked.

When your visitor visa expires, technically you can cross the border and come back again for another six months. Border agents may be concerned about the likelihood of you overstaying your visitor visa. Any documents you can provide to show that you have ties to your home country, like a job or property, make it easier to alleviate their concerns.

You'll also want to show that you have enough money in your bank account to support yourself while in Canada. If you're staying with someone during your time in Canada your expenses will be lower, but you'll need a letter from them saying that they'll be providing you with room and board.

You can also apply to extend your visitor visa, rather than making visa runs to the border. As long as you've applied to extend or change your visa before it expires, you can stay in Canada while you wait for them to make a decision thanks to implied status. If you want to spend your gap year or sabbatical hiking around Canada, this is a simple process.

The problem with life as a perpetual tourist is figuring out how to continue to support yourself without the legal right to work.

If you're staying in Canada for more than six months a year, you'll likely be considered a resident for tax purposes. You'll also need to get health insurance that covers you for your time in Canada.

An extended vacation is great if you're confident that you can use this time to decide where you want to live, get a job offer, or find a Canadian to settle down with, but it's not a long-term solution if you really want to move to Canada.

Working remotely on a tourist visa

Since I work remotely, I could have theoretically done my work while living in Canada and simply made visa runs back to the US every six months. I did work remotely while in Toronto, although I usually only spent a few weeks at a time in Canada before returning to the US. I was honest with the border agents I spoke with and let them know I would be working remotely for US companies while in Canada.

The border agents I spoke to said working remotely during my time in Canada as a tourist was okay. However, I haven't been able to find information in writing from the Canadian government confirming the legality of this. It's possible that they viewed this as falling under NAFTA's business visitor provision, which doesn't require any paperwork.

International Experience Canada

Canada has agreements with a number of countries that allow young people under the age of 35 to work for up to two years in Canada through the International Experience Canada (IEC) program.

There are actually three IEC programs:
- Travel while working with a Working Holiday
- Gain international work experience as a Young Professional
- Get work experience in your field with an International Co-op

You have to be at least 18 to apply, but the cutoff ranges from 30 to 35, depending on your nationality. You can't begin the application process until you're 18, but once you're approved you can enter Canada after you're too old to apply as long as you are selected before you age out of the program.

Here are the age cutoffs for common countries that are eligible for the IEC program:

Australia (30), Austria (30), Belgium (30), Chile (30), Costa Rica (35), Croatia (35), Czech Republic (35), Denmark (35), Estonia (35), France (35), Germany (35), Greece (35), Hong Kong (30), Ireland (35), Italy (35), Japan (30), Korea (30), Latvia (35), Lithuania (35), Mexico (29), Netherlands (30), New Zealand (35), Norway (35), Poland (35), Slovakia (35), Slovenia (35), South Korea (35), Spain (35), Sweden (30), Switzerland (35), Taiwan (35), Ukraine (35), UK (30)

Some countries are part of one IEC program, others are part of two or all three. Each participating IEC country has an annual quota of places based on reciprocal agreements with Canada. Some nationalities have their spaces fill up quickly because demand far exceeds supply.

The IEC year runs from autumn to autumn, so it's worthwhile to enter the pool as soon as it opens for the year. It's not first-come, first-served anymore, so submitting your information within the first week or two is sufficient.

Until recently, applications were processed on a first-time, first-served basis. Now there's a points system that assesses your ability to be successful in Canada. This is because Canada really wants young people to come establish a career here, so they prioritize people who would likely qualify to become permanent residents.

The length of the work permit depends on the program and your country of nationality. If you're a dual citizen you can use each passport separately, doubling your opportunities to use the program.

If your nationality isn't on the list, like the US, that means your country doesn't have a bilateral youth mobility agreement. You can still do the IEC program, but you need to apply through a recognized organization (RO). It adds to the cost, but it also means there's an organization helping you with the application, moving, and finding jobs once you arrive.

In addition to the age requirement, you'll need to show you have access to at least C$2,500, to prove you won't go broke while you're in Canada. Yes, you'll have a work permit, but presumably you'll be doing touristy things for part of the time and won't necessarily be working from the day you arrive. Don't worry, it doesn't have to be a stack of cash at the ready. You'll need a bank statement or letter from your bank issued within a week of your arrival to Canada.

Unlike other types of work permits, the IEC program does not allow you to bring your family. If your partner wishes to come, they'd need to apply for their own IEC visa.

The IEC application process

1. See if you're eligible using the Come to Canada tool on the IRCC website.
2. Use your personal reference code to create a MyCIC account. Select the option to Apply for Visitor Visa, Study, and/or Work Permit and complete your IEC profile.
   - If a field doesn't apply to you, enter N/A
   - Some countries require you be a current resident in order to apply for IEC using their bilateral agreement
   - You may need to combine multiple PDFs into one document or print, sign, and scan files for your application
   - It's advisable to print your application for your records
3. You're placed in the pool and must wait for your invitation to apply (ITA). Be sure to set up email notifications for your MyCIC account and add the email to your address book. If you do not receive an ITA, your profile expires after a year. Don't worry, you can just create a new profile until you age out of eligibility.
4. When you're sent an ITA, you must accept it within 10 days or it will expire. If it expires, you'll be put back in the pool and may be given another invitation in the future. If you have a job offer, your employer needs to submit that to the IRCC at this point.
5. Once you've accepted the ITA, you have 20 days to apply for your work permit. This is when you pay the fees for your program.
6. After submitting your work permit application, you'll be sent a request to submit biometrics. You have 30 days to submit your biometrics.
7. It takes about eight weeks for your application to be processed. You can check current processing times. If you don't hear back in eight weeks, you can request an update. If it's approved, you'll receive a Port of Entry (POE) letter in your myCIC mailbox.
8. Depending on your nationality, you may need to send your passport to the embassy to get a visa.
9. Take your POE letter with you to the airport and present it to customs when you land. The visa officer at customs will give you your work permit. You must enter Canada within 12 months of when your medical exam was done. If you don't, it expires and you'd have to start over from the beginning.

Don't buy your flight, enroll in health insurance, lease an apartment, or cut ties with your home country until you have your POE letter.

If you'd like to visit Canada as a tourist before you activate your IEC visa, you can do that. When you arrive in Canada, let the border agent know that you have an IEC permit, but you would like to enter Canada on a tourist visa and activate your IEC permit at a later date. I know several people who've done this without a problem. You'll need to leave Canada and re-enter the country when you're ready to activate your IEC permit. Just be sure to activate it before it expires.

Types of IEC permits and the selection process

There are three IEC programs: Working Holiday, Young Professionals, and International Co-op. Candidates are invited to apply in rounds based on their nationality.

Working holiday visas

Working holiday visas provide you with an open work permit, meaning you can work for anyone you'd like. Applicants are selected from the pool at random.

If you're applying for a working holiday permit and you are asked for an offer of employment number, type "A9999999" in the field. Even if you have work arranged in Canada, the working holiday visa is an open work permit, so you should not include their information.

Young Professional & International Co-op

Young Professional & International Co-op applicants will be invited to apply for a work permit as long as there are spots available. These programs require that you have a job, co-op, or internship arranged when you apply for your IEC work permit. Your permit will only be valid for that specific employer.

You can change your employer if the company has closed, you are not being paid the wages you were promised, your working conditions are unsafe, or if you have been fired. You'll need to contact the IRCC to update your permit.

If your work contract ends before your work permit does, you can renew your contract with the same employer, stay in Canada as a visitor until your permit expires, or leave Canada before your permit expires.

Documents you need for IEC

Once you're invited to apply, you have 30 days to submit your application. It can easily take more than 30 days to gather all of the paperwork, so you should start the process before getting your ITA.

International Co-op applicants must provide proof of school registration and an internship agreement outlining the position title, description of tasks to be performed, the start and end dates, the address of the internship site, and the employer's contact information.

Applicants applying through an RO must include a copy of the confirmation letter from the RO.

Needless to say, if any of the documents you submit are forged or contain false information, the IRCC will be very unhappy. Your application will be denied and you could be barred from Canada for five years.

Proof of funds

You can show you have the money to support yourself during your time in Canada by showing:
- A bank statement from the last week showing at least C$2,500
- A letter from your bank from the last week saying you have at least C$2,500 in your account
- A bank cheque for C$2,500
- Pay stubs
- Proof of a student loan providing funds
- A letter of support from the person or institution funding you

Resume

This is not a resume like you would provide to a potential employer. This is a timeline of your education, work, travel, and life in general. You want to account for all of your time, with no gaps. If you were unemployed, caring for an ill relative, or backpacking you should include that. If there are any gaps in your resume the IRCC will likely ask you for more information, which could delay your application.

Police certificate

Depending on your nationality, you'll likely need to provide a police certificate. You will need to provide a police certificate for any country you've lived in since you turned 18, including any country where you spend more than six months in a row.

When including multiple certificates, you'll need to provide them all in one document, as there is only one upload field.

Getting a police certificate can take a very long time. You can upload your receipt or a screenshot of the confirmation page as proof that you've requested the police certificate and they'll provide you with a new deadline.

Medical exam

Not every applicant requires a medical exam. This depends on what type of job you're applying for and if you've lived in or traveled to certain countries.

If you need a medical exam, you have to go to a panel physician. They'll give you a form for you to upload with your application. If you can't get a medical exam before your 30 days are up, you can upload proof that you've scheduled one.

Digital photo

You must provide a passport photo that meets IRCC specifications. They are very fussy about this, so make sure you follow instructions carefully.

Passport and/or travel documents

Your work permit will only be issued for as long as your passport is valid. You also need at least one blank page in your passport, other than the last page.

Visitor visa application

If you come from a country that requires visitor visas, you'll need to apply for a visitor visa. You will automatically get an eTA once your work permit application is approved. If you leave and re-enter Canada, check to make sure your eTA is still valid.

Letter of explanation

If you were unable to provide all documentation by the deadline through no fault of your own, you can write a letter of explanation and ask for the deadline to be extended or for the requirement to be waived. It's important to provide whatever proof you can that you requested the documents (such as a police certificate) in a timely manner.

You have the option of including a letter of explanation with your application. Some people find that the system requires this, due to a bug. To get around this, you can upload a blank document and then delete it before submission.

Biometrics

You are now required to submit biometrics: a photo and fingerprints. This must be done at a Visa Application Centre (VAC) or Application Support

Centre (ASC). There are no VACs or ASCs in Canada, so if you are applying from within Canada you'll need to leave the country to do this. This was not required prior to 2018. The IRCC has a tool to help you determine if you need to provide biometrics.

You are responsible for getting yourself to a VAC or ASC and paying C$85 to have the biometrics done.

Arriving in Canada

When you arrive in Canada, you'll need to provide the following documents to a border services officer:

- Your passport
- Your POE letter
- Proof of funds
- Proof of health insurance
- A ticket to leave Canada at the end of your stay or proof of funds to purchase a ticket.
- If you are doing an unpaid co-op, you may be asked to provide proof of enough money to support yourself for the entire time.

You can be refused entry into Canada if you're missing any of these documents.

If you are bringing C$10k or more across the border with you, you must declare this to the border services officer. You may be asked to show proof of where the money came from.

If you've lost your POE letter, Canada is very nice and will give you a new one.

Your health insurance must be valid for your entire stay. It needs to cover medical care, hospitalization, and repatriation. If your insurance coverage ends before your expected stay, your work permit will expire when your insurance does. A provincial health card will not meet this requirement.

When you've been given your work permit, check it over carefully before you leave the international zone. Check the bilateral agreement between Canada and your country of nationality to make sure the length of your work permit is correct. Make sure your work location is correct. If you are doing a working holiday, it should say "open."

If there's a mistake on the permit, tell a border services officer immediately. If there's a mistake it's much more difficult (or impossible) to fix it once you leave.

Planning your trip

You're responsible for everything about planning your time in Canada, from completing the application to finding a job and getting a place to stay. If you'd like to have help organizing these details, you can work with a RO.

Costs

- International Experience Canada: C$150
- Working Holiday: additional C$100
- Young Professional & International Co-op: your employer must pay a C$230 compliance fee and submit your offer of employment to IRCC before you submit your work permit application.

Additional paperwork

These are the costs for New York City, so they'll vary depending on where you're living when you apply.
- Police certificate: $18
- Fingerprinting: $25
- Medical exam: $350
- Passport photos: $20
- Biometrics: C$85

Staying in Canada after your IEC permit expires

You cannot renew or extend your IEC work permit. Some countries allow you to participate multiple times. You may also be eligible to get a work permit through another program.

If you're applying for a new work permit, you must apply at least 30 days before your current work permit expires.

You may be able to extend your stay in Canada as a visitor after your work permit expires. You need to do this before your work permit expires. If you're from a country that doesn't require visas to visit Canada and the US, you can also simply cross from Canada into the US and re-enter Canada as a tourist.

After a year of working in Canada, you might be eligible to apply for permanent resident status through the Express Entry Canadian Experience (CEC) program. You might have also fallen in love with a Canadian (hopefully they love you back) or have decided to stay and go back to university or perfect your French. All of these can get you a new work permit or PR status.

Studying in Canada

Attending a university, training program, or language school in Canada doesn't just get you a great education, it also puts you on the pathway to Canadian citizenship.

Acceptance into a designated learning institution in Canada makes you eligible for a study permit. You don't have to go back to school for a university degree in order to qualify, many vocational schools and language schools can also get you a student visa.

Not all schools in Canada are approved by the government to qualify you for a student visa, so make sure your school is on the list before you apply. If your school loses its designated learning institution status, you can complete your current study permit term, but you can't renew it unless you change schools.

Any programs that are six months or less will simply have you enter on a tourist visa, so be sure that both your school and your program qualify for a visa.

You need an acceptance letter from the school first before you can apply for a study permit. Your school will walk you through the permit application process.

Student Direct Stream

If you are currently living in and a citizen of China, India, Vietnam or the Philippines, the Student Direct Stream provides faster visa application processing times.

In order to participate, you will need to:

- have been accepted to a designated learning institution and pay your first year of tuition
- have a score of 6 on the IELTS or a 7 in the Test d'évaluation de français (TEF)
- have a Guaranteed Investment Certificate (GIC) of C$10k
- get your medical exam
- get your police certificate

If you don't qualify for the Student Direct Stream, you can still apply through the regular study permit process.

What your study permit includes

Once approved for a study permit, you'll be able to live in Canada for the length of your educational program, plus an additional six months after your program is completed.

Your student visa will allow you to bring your spouse (or common law partner) and your kids with you. Your spouse or partner can even apply for an open work permit for the length of your student visa.

As a student, you can apply for a work permit, too. Because you need to be enrolled in classes full-time in order to qualify for a study permit, you can work up to 20 hours a week while school is in session and full-time during breaks.

Your learning institution will report your academic status to the IRCC, so make sure you stay in good academic standing in order to keep your study permit (and any associated work permits) from being cancelled.

After you complete your studies

Once you complete your studies, you can apply for a post graduation work permit. There are specific criteria you need to meet in order to be eligible for a post graduation work permit, so keep this in mind.

You have to apply before your student visa expires and have maintained full-time student status for the duration of your program, among other requirements. Your post graduation work permit can be valid for as long as three years, so be sure to plan ahead and not miss the opportunity to take advantage of this.

The most common route from student visa to Canadian citizenship is to use the post graduation work permit to get the experience required for Express Entry's Canadian Experience Class. Most Canadian graduates will qualify for Express Entry after a year of working full-time.

If you already have professional experience from outside of Canada, you may be eligible for Express Entry as soon as you graduate.

There are lots of Provincial Nomination Programs that encourage you to stay in Canada after you graduate from a Canadian university. These change depending on the needs of each province and the whims of politics. If you've earned your Masters or PhD at a Canadian university, but don't qualify for Express Entry or are short on points, check with your province to see if they'll nominate you to become a permanent resident. Your university will have information on the current programs.

Working in Canada

Many people assume that the easiest way to move to Canada is by getting a job offer or that you need a job offer in order to move to Canada. As you know by now, this isn't the case. If you're a young professional or work in a skilled trade, you can probably move to Canada as a permanent resident through Express Entry.

Your odds of finding a company to sponsor you for a temporary work permit vary greatly, based on your professional experience and personal network.

If you do find a company to sponsor you, their attorney will take care of getting you a work permit. Some small businesses will try to get you to do this work, but they're the ones who have to apply, not you.

Unlike some countries, getting a temporary work permit issued can happen in a matter of weeks. You might want to start packing as soon as you accept the job offer.

One interesting detail is that you can't get a work permit for any employer "who, on a regular basis, offers striptease, erotic dance, escort services or erotic massages." That suggests they're banned from hiring foreign workers, even if you're doing the accounting. Blame sex trafficking.

Labour Market Impact Assessment

Your prospective employer will need to get a Labour Market Impact Assessment (LMIA) to show that they couldn't hire a Canadian for the job and that hiring you won't have a negative impact on the economy.

You'll need to submit:

- your application,
- the job offer letter,
- a copy of the LMIA or offer of employment number,
- proof of experience or education, based on the job requirements,
- an eTA or visitor visa, if you need one

They can do this all online. You may be required to have an interview with an IRCC official and/or get a medical exam. If your job requires a medical exam, it can add significantly to the processing time.

Mobilité Francophone

The Francophone mobility program is an exception to the requirement to get a LMIA. If you are fluent in French and have a job offer outside of Quebec, this is an easy pathway to getting a temporary work permit. The job must be at a National Occupation Code (NOC) skill level of 0, A or B, but the job does not have to be performed in French. Whether or not a language exam is required is at the discretion of the visa officer.

Your work permit application will use LMIA exemption code C16. Because you do not need a LMIA, the $1,000 LMIA application fee is not required under the Mobilité Francophone program.

Prior to September 2017, you were only eligible for this program if you were recruited through a government job fair abroad. While Canadian government offices abroad continue to recruit French speaking foreign workers for this program, you no longer need to be recruited at an event to be eligible.

Entering Canada

Once your application is approved, you'll get a letter of introduction. When you arrive at the port of entry, you'll show this to a border services officer. Hopefully they'll give you a work permit without any trouble. Sometimes they'll ask for piles of documentation. This is at the discretion of the border agent. I know people who've only gotten their work permit after going back for additional documents three times! Other times they approve work permits without looking at anything.

Your work permit will be specific to your employer and will say how long it's valid for. It may even specify what location you can work at if your company has multiple locations.

Free trade agreements

Thanks to NAFTA and the future USMCA, citizens of the USA and Mexico have access to special work permits in Canada. While the USMCA includes a provision to revisit the agreement every six years and a 16 year sunset clause, it doesn't look like these aspects of the agreement will be discontinued any time soon.

Canada has other free trade agreements with labor mobility provisions modeled on NAFTA with Chile, Peru, Columbia, South Korea and is a participant in the General Agreement on Trade in Services (GATS). Thus, this may apply to you, even if you're not a citizen of the US or Mexico.

The North American Free Trade Agreement (NAFTA) is in the process of being replaced by the United States–Mexico–Canada Agreement (USMCA). As of July 2019, only Mexico has ratified the agreement, although all three countries have signed it. NAFTA remains in effect until USMCA is ratified by Canada and the US. This all makes little difference to you, as the labor mobility provisions regarding business visitors, professionals, intra-company transferees, traders, and investors between the three countries remain unchanged from NAFTA to USMCA.

Getting a TN visa is much simpler, and faster, than getting a temporary work permit. In fact, under NAFTA you may not even require a work permit in order to work in Canada if you're conducting certain types of business or are involved in trading and investing.

You can get a TN visa at the port of entry. Remember that even with a TN visa, you can be denied entry at the border if an agent determines that you are inadmissible.

Working in Canada under NAFTA doesn't provide a direct pathway to stay in Canada permanently. However, you can get a new TN visa every three years. There is no limit to how many times you can get a TN visa. Your time working in Canada under a TN visa can also make you eligible to apply for permanent resident status.

Business visitors

Most business visitors are only in Canada for a few days, but you can stay for up to six months without needing a work permit, thanks to NAFTA. You can spend time in Canada looking for ways to grow your business, making investments, or building business relationships. Conferences, meetings, and standard business training or support are all fine.

Whenever I travelled to Canada as a business visitor, I made sure to have a letter from my employer briefly explaining what I was doing and for how long. No one ever asked me for the letter, but being overly prepared is my style. Taking a couple minutes to get the papers together seemed better than potentially being denied entry at the border.

While no one ever asked to see my paperwork, they would ask me basic questions about who the meetings were with and when they were taking place. They'd ask to see my business card and quiz me about what it is I do. They don't really care about your work, they're just making sure you're being truthful about your intentions. If your job is difficult to explain, keep it simple. Yes, you want to be honest, but you also don't want to accidentally end up spending your whole day at customs because you got too in-depth and set off red flags for no reason.

Border agents want to know that you aren't going to stay longer than six months and that your main source of income is outside of Canada. Finding a few new Canadian clients is fine. Of course, they may ask for proof that you have funds to support yourself during your stay, like pay stubs, W-2s, or bank account statements. Having a return flight booked never hurts.

Professionals

To be a professional under NAFTA, you still have to jump through some hoops. Why is it worth it? As a professional, whatever company is hiring you doesn't need to get approval from the Employment and Social Development Canada to hire you.

In order to qualify, you need to have experience working one of the jobs mentioned in NAFTA or the future USMCA. NAFTA and the USMCA state what sort of degrees or licenses you need to demonstrate your qualifications. You also need to have a written job offer.

You won't be surprised to hear that anyone working in medicine or science will probably see themselves on this list. College or seminary instructors are in the clear. Quite a few general business people are on there, including graphic designers, librarians, landscape architects, social workers, and hotel managers.

The final step is to get a work permit. You can apply online and the IRCC even walks you through the steps. You get your actual work permit at the border, which can be a little anxiety inducing.

While the type of work I do shows up on the NAFTA list, getting a written job offer from a Canadian employer wasn't so easy. Several companies let me know during the phone interview that they were not interested in hiring someone who wasn't a resident, even if they didn't need to get an LMIA. In spite of having gone on a several interviews, I was a permanent resident before getting any job offers. However, I didn't put much effort into this, since I was pretty sure I could keep my current job, which is what I ultimately did.

The amount of effort required to find a company willing to hire someone on a TN visa varies greatly depending on your industry and personal factors.

Intra-company transferees

Does your company have an office in Canada? If you've worked there for a year and can convince them to transfer you, you're good to go.

You'll need to be working as a manager or a specialist and you'll still need a work permit. You can apply online and the IRCC walks you through the steps.

Traders and investors

If your company is involved in a significant amount of trade between the US and Canada, you can stay for up to six months. Your company's attorney can advise you on the NAFTA rules you'll need to meet and the process for getting a work permit.

Parent & grandparent super visa

If you want to live in Canada temporarily and are parent or grandparent of a Canadian citizen or permanent resident, you can apply for a super visa. This will allow you to live in Canada for up to two years at a time over the course of 10 years.

A super visa doesn't last forever and you'll have to prove that you plan to return to your home country at the end of your stay. The application takes 20 months or so to process.

In order for your child or grandchild to sponsor your super visa, they will need to meet certain income criteria to prove that they will be able to support you financially. This is the case, even if you can support yourself. You will also need to pass a medical exam and have valid Canadian insurance coverage for at least a year. You won't be eligible for provincial health insurance.

The super visa will not allow you to work in Canada, nor will it grant you permanent residency. You will need to leave Canada at the end of the visa unless you're sponsored to become a permanent resident under the family class program.

Visiting with the intent to stay

Lots of people think you can just show up at the border with all of your worldly possessions and stay. If you do it right, that's actually an option.

This is called "dual intent." You're entering Canada as a visitor with a plan to change your visa type during your stay.

The thing is, border agents are responsible for figuring out who is a risk of overstaying their visa and preventing them from entering the country in the first place. Someone asking for a visitor visa who is clearly planning on staying for longer than six months is obviously at a very high risk of overstaying their visa. Thus, the border agent will only allow you to enter Canada if it is abundantly clear that you:

- qualify for permanent resident status,
- actually intend to go through the legal process to become a permanent resident, and
- can support yourself (or be supported by your spouse) for at least a year, including private health insurance.

Most people who enter Canada with dual intent are being sponsored for PR by their Canadian spouse. You can request a "visitor record" to extend your visitor visa from six months to a year, giving you more time to process your application.

Being able to answer questions about the immigration process and provide documentation to show that you qualify for PR goes far in demonstrating your honest intentions to follow the law.

Remember, being allowed to enter Canada as a visitor with dual intent is at the discretion of the border agent.

Part Four: Immigrating to Canada

You're done with the expat life and you want to stay. There are two main paths for permanent resident status in Canada: your family and your career. There are several different programs for each of those pathways.

Immigrating to Canada is fairly straightforward. It involves a pretty significant amount of paperwork, all of which will need to be scanned and uploaded to the IRCC website or mailed in as a paper application. While the process is tedious, it's not difficult.

If you aren't moving to Canada because of family, you're most likely immigrating using the Express Entry system. I'll go over this in excruciating detail in part five.

Spousal Sponsorship

The bad news is that being married to a Canadian doesn't automatically get a you a Canadian passport. You'll have to submit numerous documents to the IRCC to apply for permanent resident status, assuming you qualify.

The good news is you don't even need to be legally married for a Canadian partner to sponsor you for PR status.

Of course, your dependent children are included on your application, so if you are approved for PR status, they are, too. Just remember that you don't actually become a permanent resident until you arrive at a port of entry, declare yourself a landed immigrant, and are approved. Each person on your application needs to do this before your landing paperwork expires.

Before you start getting the paperwork together and planning your move, remember that you still need to be admissible to Canada and your partner needs to be eligible to sponsor you.

This process was completely redesigned in December 2016, tweaked twice in 2017, and significantly updated on Valentines Day of 2018 (because the IRCC has a sense of humor). Given all the changes, there's lots of conflicting and confusing information out there.

Can your Canadian love sponsor you?

Not just anyone can sponsor you to become a permanent resident of Canada, even if you're married. In order to sponsor you, your partner must:

- Be over the age of 18
- Not be receiving social assistance, other than disability
- Meet income requirements
- Not be in jail, bankrupt, or have been convicted of a violent crime
- Not have sponsored another spouse in the last three years or failed to support a spouse or child they sponsored
- Have paid their taxes and any court judgements (like child support and alimony)

If your partner is a Canadian permanent resident, they need to be living in Canada when they sponsor you. If they came to Canada through spousal sponsorship or family sponsorship themselves, they need to have been a permanent resident for at least five years.

If your partner is a Canadian citizen, they can be living anywhere in the world while they sponsor you, but you must plan on living in Canada together once your application is approved.

Your sponsor also needs to be willing to make a legally binding promise that they will provide for you for a certain amount of time, called an

Undertaking. The specifics of this guarantee depend on your relationship and where in Canada you will be moving to.

No country likes sham marriages. You'll need to be able to provide documents to prove that you're in a bona fide relationship. If you've been married for a decade and have kids, great. If you've been living together forever and are financially entangled, great. If you just met on Maple Match, you'll face additional scrutiny. The decision is at the discretion of immigration agents.

Governments tend to have outdated notions of what commitment looks like. Many couples maintain separate bank accounts, don't add their partner to the lease, and otherwise lack the sort of paper trail the IRCC will look for. You might want to take some steps now to make sure you will have some government approved proof you're really together. Minimally, make sure you take some photos of both of you together on your next vacation.

Previously, people who were sponsored by their partners and had been in a relationship for less than two years were required to live with their partners for two years once they arrived in Canada or face having their permanent resident status revoked. This is no longer the case.

You do not need to stay in an abusive relationship in order to maintain your status in Canada and there are organizations to help you find a safe living situation.

There are three types of relationships that will allow someone to bring you to Canada through spousal sponsorship: marriage, common law partnerships, and conjugal partnerships.

Marriage

Are you and your partner legally married? Great, that makes things easier. Canada will recognize your marriage as long as:
- it's legally recognized in the country where it took place,
- it's legally recognized in Canada, and
- both partners were physically present for the marriage ceremony.

If the country you were married in repealed marriage equality or no longer recognizes your marriage for whatever reason, you can either get re-married in a country that will recognize it or apply as common law partners.

Common law partnerships

If you've been in a committed relationship with your partner for two years and have lived together for at least 12 consecutive months, you can apply for spousal sponsorship as common law partners.

If you have children together, you still have to live together for a year before you're eligible, but the two year requirement is waived.

This is a great option for people in same-sex relationships in a country that doesn't recognize marriage equality. It's also a great option for people who want to stay together badly enough to move to another country, but not badly enough to put a ring on it.

You'll need to provide documentation showing that your love is real and that you shared a home and finances. Partners who aren't legally married are more likely to face IRCC scrutiny.

Conjugal partnerships

Sometimes there are extenuating circumstances preventing you and your partner from getting married or living together. You can still apply for spousal sponsorship as conjugal partners.

You'll need to provide documentation showing that you and your partner were unable to live together for 12 consecutive months due to immigration barriers, religious reasons, or sexual orientation. These reasons must be beyond your control.

While family responsibilities or a tough job market are a significant hurdle to living together, they wouldn't be enough to qualify you as conjugal partners. This is primarily for people coming from countries with laws against homosexuality or facing other serious legal logistical challenges.

Fiancé visas

Canada used to have a fiance visa so partners could move to Canada while planning their wedding. This is no longer an option.

If you are planning your wedding and would like your partner to move to Canada prior to the wedding, I'll let you in on a secret: lots of people don't get legally married on their "wedding day." You can get married legally and hold a ceremony after your sponsorship has been approved.

You can also try moving to Canada using dual intent, but this means you might have to re-plan your wedding if the border agent turns you away.

Which is better: spousal sponsorship or being a skilled worker?

Immigration through spousal sponsorship isn't any faster than immigrating through the skilled worker program. Just like spousal sponsorship doesn't require you to be married, the skilled worker program doesn't require you to have a job offer.

Why would you want to use the skilled worker program, Express Entry, rather than spousal sponsorship?

- Your spouse isn't eligible to sponsor you
- You have been married a short time, don't have kids, and don't have strong documentation to support that you're in a committed relationship
- You'd rather the IRCC scrutinize your work history than your love letters

Prior to 2018, the application processing time was significantly faster for Express Entry. That's no longer the case.

How spousal sponsorship works in Canada

Types of spousal sponsorship

There are two types of spousal sponsorship, which are based on where you're living while your application is processed.

In Canada Class

If you and your Canadian partner are already living in Canada, you're eligible to apply as Spouse in Canada. This is the case if you have a valid visa as a visitor, student, or worker.

This allows you to apply for an open work permit while you wait for your PR application to go through. You cannot work legally until your open work permit application has been approved. It is an especially bad idea to work illegally while the government is digging into your personal life.

Once you have an open work permit, you'll likely be eligible to register for provincial medical insurance.

Make sure whatever visa you're on doesn't expire before your application is approved. You can apply to extend your current visa while your application is being processed.

If you leave Canada while your application is being processed, there is no guarantee that you will be allowed back into the country. Is it likely that border agents won't let you back in? Not terribly, but be sure to decide if it's worth the risk before you leave Canada.

Family Class

If you're living outside of Canada, you'll need to be sponsored under Family Class. Your application will be processed by the visa office in the country you're currently living in.

If you're planning on moving out of Canada temporarily while your application is being processed or the processing times for your country are faster than in Canada, you may want to apply through Family Class, even if you qualify for In Canada processing.

While waiting, you should be able to visit Canada under a regular visitor visa with dual intent. Dual intent is when you're entering Canada on one visa (like a tourist visa) while also applying for another type of visa (such as permanent resident status). You may face additional questions at the port of entry, but in most cases it just adds a few minutes to your travel time.

If you're feeling particularly brave, you can even see if you can move to Canada to live with your spouse while waiting for your application to process. This is totally up to the border agent on duty, so be prepared to be turned away. You'd have to demonstrate that:

- Your partner has submitted your sponsorship application
- You totally qualify and understand how the process works
- You'll leave Canada if your application is denied
- You won't work illegally while you wait for your application to process
- You can support yourself (or your partner will support you) while you wait
- You have private medical insurance coverage

The border agent will decide how long your visa will be valid for and you'll need to make sure you don't overstay this visa. You may also have issues bringing your things across the border before your application is approved, depending on what visa you're currently on.

Quebec sponsorship

If your sponsor is living in Quebec or you plan on living in Quebec when your application is approved, the IRCC will direct you to apply for a CSQ from MIDI once they've completed processing your federal application. See the section on Quebec for more information on this process.

Documents checklist

Your immigration application requires extensive documentation of your relationship, as well as lots of information about you. Any documents that aren't in English or French will need to be translated.

The exact documents required depends on your relationship to your sponsor, your country of residence, and the countries your key documents come from. The IRCC provides you with a custom document checklist for your specific situation.

If you can't submit a document included in the IRCC checklist, you must include a detailed explanation of why you can't submit this document or your application will be returned to you for being incomplete. If you have a legitimate reason for being unable to provide a document, the IRCC will work with you to provide alternate documentation or waive the requirement.

Be sure to sign any places where signatures are required. The IRCC checklist provides a list of places where you need to sign. If you forget a signature the IRCC will return the application to you without processing it.

Documents verifying your relationship

- Proof of cohabitation if you are currently living together.
- If you are not living together:
  - As much proof as possible to demonstrate the reasons why you have not been able to share a household and/or finances
  - 10 pages of printed media to demonstrate ongoing communication (letters, text messages, social media posts, and/or emails)
  - Proof of visitation (plane tickets or boarding passes and passport pages)
- If you are married: marriage certificate and 20 photographs from your wedding
- If you are in a common law or conjugal relationship: as much information as possible to demonstrate that you share a home and finances such as:
  - Statements for joint bank accounts or credit cards
  - Mortgage documents signed by both parties
  - Property lease signed by both of you
  - Property ownership documents in both of your names
  - Declarations from people verifying your relationship
  - Pictures from your lives demonstrating that your relationship is genuine such as from vacations, family events, holidays, etc.
- Birth certificates of any children that you have together
- Proof of three of the things below (not needed if you have been together for more than 2 years, currently live together, have children together, and have only been married to each other):
  - Joint ownership or lease of a home
  - Joint responsibility of utilities
  - Government issued identification documents showing the same address
  - Evidence of financial support between you and your spouse
  - Proof that your relationship is recognized by your friends and family (such as social media posts showing that your relationship is public, cards mailed to you for your wedding or anniversary, wedding photos)

Documents your sponsor will need to provide

- Proof of citizenship (Canadian birth certificate, certificate of citizenship, or Canadian passport) or permanent residency (permanent resident card, record of landing, or confirmation of permanent residence (CoPR)
- Proof of income:
  - Tax returns and income slips for most recent tax year OR explanation for why you cannot provide these
  - Letter from your employer stating length of employment, salary, and hours per week (if applicable)
  - Welfare receipts and/or receipts from government payouts (if applicable)
- Required only if you will be immigrating with your children:
  - Sponsorship evaluation
  - Evidence of income for the previous 12 months
  - Evidence of savings that show they meet the financial requirements
  - Financial evaluation if you are the parent to a dependent child with a child of their own
- Required only if they have been married to another person: divorce, annulment, separation, or death certificate
- Application to sponsor, sponsorship agreement and undertaking
- Sponsorship evaluation and relationship questionnaire form

Pledge of financial support

Your partner will have to sign a contract promising to financially support you for three years, known as an Undertaking. This includes food, shelter, clothing, household supplies, personal items, and any healthcare costs not covered by provincial health insurance. They must also meet minimum income requirements. Your income does not count toward the income requirement.

If you are immigrating to Canada with dependent children who are not related to your Canadian partner, your partner will need to pledge support your children for ten years or until the child is 22 years old (whichever happens first).

If a dependent child included in your application has children of their own, you must include a Financial Evaluation (IMM 1283) form.

If you or your children (not related to your Canadian partner) apply for social assistance during those years, your spouse will need to repay that amount to the Canadian government, even if you are separated or divorced.

While you don't have to meet any financial requirements, you'll need to sign a pledge promising you will make all reasonable efforts to support yourself and your children once you are legally able to work.

Documents you will need to provide

Your Identification
- Valid passport
- Birth certificates for you and
- 2 photographs for permanent resident card
- Police certificate(s) from any country that you have lived in for 6+ months since turning 18
    - Some countries require a consent form before issuing a police certificate. If you need a police certificate from one of these countries, you submit the consent form to the IRCC in place of the police certificate and the IRCC will then request a police certificate from that country on your behalf
- Required only if you have been married to another person: divorce, annulment, separation, or death certificate
- Required only if you are applying through the Spouse or common law Partner in Canada Class: visa or permit confirming that you are currently allowed to legally live in Canada
- Required only if you have dependent children (even if they will not be immigrating with you): birth certificates, certificates of adoption, or custody papers
- If you are not currently living in Canada, you will need to provide biometrics
    - If you have opted to have your application processed overseas, you will need to provide biometrics, even if you are currently living in Canada
    - You will need to give your biometrics, even if you gave biometrics previously for another application
    - Anyone included on your application will also need to provide biometrics. You cannot get your biometrics done until you get a biometric instruction letter (BIL) from the IRCC

Forms
- Schedule A – Background/Declaration [eIMM 5669]: This form is submitted first
- Relationship information and sponsorship evaluation form [IMM 5532 E]
- Generic application for Canada [IMM 0008]

- Application to Sponsor, Sponsorship Agreement and Undertaking [IMM 1344]: A copy of this form must be included for each person on the application
- Additional Family Information [IMM 5406]: If a dependent child on your application has one or more children of their own
- Declaration From Non-Accompanying Parent/Guardian For Minors Immigrating to Canada [IMM 5604]: If a child included in your application has a parent besides you and the person sponsoring you, you must submit this form, along with a copy of the other parent's photo ID. If this is not possible, you must include a letter of explanation
- Use of Representative form [IMM 5476]: If you have an immigration attorney or consultant preparing your application

The application

When submitting your application, be sure to have submitted the exact documents required by the IRCC in the checklist they provided, based on your specific situation. You can complete the forms online and then mail in printed copies for the paper section of the application.

When filling out the application:

- You must complete every field of the application. Do not leave a section blank, write "N/A."
- If you don't know a complete date of birth, use an asterisk in the field for the year, month, or day that you don't know.
- If you don't have a family name or given name on your passport or travel document, type "N/A" in the corresponding application field.
- Write addresses in full without using any abbreviations.
- If you need more space, you can attach additional sheets.
- Be sure to sign and date where it is required. If someone under 18 is required to sign, a parent or guardian should sign in their place.
- Your custom document checklist should be the first page when you mail in your application.
- If you are applying for an open work permit, the application for this and proof of payment should be included after the document checklist.
- Several forms have the option to validate their completeness (IMM 1344, IMM 0008, and eIMM 5669). If a validated form provides a barcode, you should print this out and include it beneath the checklist page in your application. If you are applying for an open work permit, the barcodes go after your work permit application.

- Supporting documents (or letters of explanation) should be provided in the order provided in the IRCC document checklist.
- If they require an original document, be sure to provide an original and not a copy.
- Your paper application cannot be stapled, in a folder, in a binder, or in a plastic sleeve. You may use paper clips to keep photographs from getting lost in the envelope.

Your sponsor will get a confirmation of receipt once they've submitted the complete application. You can sign up for notifications about the status of your application, as well as check online.

Your eligibility

Back in 2018 the IRCC switched the order of things to weed out applications that will ultimately be denied a little bit faster.

First, they review your eligibility to become a permanent resident of Canada. This part of the application is done on paper, using the Schedule A – Background/Declaration (IMM 5669) form and police certificates. This needs to be mailed to Mississauga or Sydney.

While the application is on paper, your fees must be paid online.

Your medical exam can't be done by just any doctor, it needs to be done by a panel physician approved by the IRCC, so follow instructions carefully. You also probably need to supply biometrics, which needs to be done in person at an approved location.

While the initial application is done on paper, you can still link it to an online account. Your online account gives you the ability to communicate with the IRCC online, rather than through the postal system. The IRCC provides instruction on how to link your application to your account after you create an account or sign in. They also have an FAQ to help if you encounter any problems creating or linking your account.

Your sponsor's eligibility

Once you've been approved, the IRCC will evaluate your partner's eligibility to sponsor you.

The IRCC may ask for additional documents or even require an interview. If they require an interview, you can request that it take place at the visa office closest to you. Even though they try to accommodate your requests, this will likely still require traveling because there aren't a lot of visa offices.

Where to mail your application

Regular mail
Application for spouses, common-law partners or conjugal partners outside Canada and all dependent child sponsorships (including if you are living in Canada but choosing overseas sponsorship):
CPC Sydney
P.O. Box 9500
Sydney, NS
B1P 0H5

Application for spouses or common-law partners currently living in Canada applying under the Spouse or Common-Law Partner in Canada class:
CPC Mississauga
P.O. Box 5040, Station B
Mississauga, ON
L5A 3A4

By courier
Application for spouses, common-law partners or conjugal partners outside Canada and all dependent child sponsorships (including if you are living in Canada but choosing overseas sponsorship):
CPC Sydney
49 Dorchester Street
Sydney, NS
B1P 5Z2

Application for spouses or common-law partners currently living in Canada applying under the Spouse or Common-Law Partner in Canada class:
CPC Mississauga
2 Robert Speck Parkway, Suite 300
Mississauga, ON
L4Z 1H8

Quebec sponsorship
If your sponsor is living in Quebec or you plan on living in Quebec when your application is approved, the IRCC will direct you to apply for a CSQ from MIDI once they've completed processing your federal application. See the section on Quebec for more information.

After you submit your application

The IRCC aims to process applications within a year. The IRCC website lists current processing times. If your application is incomplete or requires extra scrutiny, it can take much longer.

- It is important to keep your contact information up to date.
- If you create an online account and link it to your application, all updates will be sent through that.
    - If you have a representative, your representative can link their account to your application, but you cannot.
    - I found that automated emails from the myCIC system were often filtered as spam. You want to set up a filter rule to make sure emails from donotreply@cic.gc.ca would be marked as important to make sure you don't miss any important messages.
- If you provide an email on your application and don't have an online account, they'll contact you via email. If you hand write your application forms and they are unable to read your email address, they will use your postal address.
- If you don't have an online account and don't provide an email address, they will contact you through the mailing address you provided on your application.
- If you apply using a representative, that person will receive all correspondence.
- If you authorize your sponsor to act as your representative, they will receive all correspondence.

Approval

Once your application is approved, you'll get a Confirmation of Permanent Residence (CoPR). This document will have an expiration date. You have to go to a Canadian port of entry or visa office and declare yourself a landed immigrant before this expiration date.

If you don't declare landing and change your status before it expires, you'd have to start the whole process over again. Everyone on your application must become a permanent resident before their CoPR expires.

Once you've landed, you'll get your permanent resident card in the mail within a few weeks. You'll be eligible to apply for provincial health insurance, if you aren't already covered.

Deemed ineligible

If your partner is found ineligible to be a sponsor, the IRCC will return your application and refund your fees. You can appeal this decision or resolve the issue and reapply.

Sponsoring a family member

Canada's Family Class program is designed to allow Canadians to bring their dependent children, parents, and grandparents to the country as new permanent residents. The process for sponsoring a dependent child is the same as sponsoring a spouse. The process of sponsoring parents and grandparents is detailed below.

In order to sponsor another type of family member, a sponsor must prove that they don't have any family members in Canada and have no living immediate family members (a spouse or dependent child) that they could sponsor.

If you're approved for permanent resident status through family sponsorship, you can bring your spouse (including a common law partner) and dependent children with you, so long as you include them on your application.

Sponsoring a dependent child

The process for sponsoring a dependent child is the same as sponsoring a spouse. Sponsoring a child you adopt internationally is slightly different.

Sponsoring immediate family members after you receive PR

Until recently, immediate family members who were not declared on your application for permanent residence were banned from family class sponsorship in the future, since applicants had omitted key information and this was viewed as committing fraud.

However, the IRCC determined that family members were being omitted because of gender discrimination, power imbalances within relationships, and complex family situations. Thus, there's a pilot program that will allow previously ineligible family members to be sponsored. This is planned to run from September 9, 2019, to September 9, 2021.

If you included a family member on your PR application but indicated they were not accompanying you to Canada or they were granted a CoPR and did not immigrate before it expired, you may sponsor them through the regular family reunification program without needing to rely on this pilot program.

Parent and Grandparent Program

If you are the parent or grandparent of a Canadian citizen or permanent resident, they can apply to sponsor your immigration through the Parent and

Grandparent Program (PGP). Only 10,000 people are invited to apply each year through a lottery system.

First, you need to submit an Interest to Sponsor form through the IRCC website. All applicants that expressed interest will be notified even if they are not invited to apply. If you're selected, your sponsor will be invited to complete the full application for the Parent and Grandparent Program within 60 days. That's not enough time to get the documents required, so you'll want to begin collecting documents ahead of time.

Due to the number of applications received, it's estimated that this lottery system gives each applicant a 20% chance of getting selected. Those that aren't selected are allowed to re-apply the following year.

For the applications that are approved, Canada aims to process the immigration process within a year.

In spite of whatever finances you have yourself, your child or grandchild that sponsors you will need to demonstrate that they have the means to support you for a period of 20 years.

Document checklist

Forms
- Application to sponsor, sponsorship agreement, and undertaking
- Financial evaluation for parents and grandparents
- Income sources for the sponsorship of parents and grandparents (if applicable)
- Statutory declaration of common-law union (if applicable)
- Generic application form for Canada
- Additional dependants declaration
- Background declaration
- Additional family information
- Use of representative (if applicable)
- Copy of fee payment receipt

Supporting documents
- Sponsor's ID and proof of citizenship or PR status
- Spouse's ID and proof of citizenship or PR status (if applicable)
- Proof of applicant's relationship to sponsor
- Copy of passport for applicant and dependents
- Proof of relationship for applicant's dependents
- Two photos of applicant and all dependents (to IRCC specifications)

Sponsoring Other Family Members

In order to sponsor you, your family member would have to demonstrate that they:

- Have no spouse or common law partner
- Have no living parents or grandparents anywhere in the world
- Have no relatives living in Canada, including: children, parents, grandparents, siblings, uncles, aunts, nieces, or nephews

If that's the case, they can sponsor you if you're a sibling, uncle, aunt, niece, or nephew.

If they have no living close relatives, then they could apply to sponsor you if you're relative related by blood or adoption, such as a cousin.

Requirements for your sponsor

Your family member must be over the age of 18 and currently living in Canada. None of the following conditions can apply to them:

- Have ever received government financial assistance (other than disability)
- Defaulted on a court-ordered support order (alimony, child support)
- Have been convicted of a violent or sexual crime
- Defaulted on an immigration loan
- Is currently in prison
- Is in bankruptcy
- Has sponsored another family member for immigration but failed to financially support them

Financial requirements

While you are expected to make all attempts to support yourself once you become a resident of Canada, your family member must promise to support you financially for 10-20 years.

- Parent or grandparent: 20 years
- Any other family member: 10 years

They'll need to meet certain income requirements in order to be eligible to sponsor you. They'll have to promise to provide basic requirements including food, clothing, utilities, shelter, fuel, household supplies, as well as health care not covered by the provincial health care system, such as vision and dental care. They are still financially responsible for you during this time, even if you become estranged.

Quebec sponsorship

If your sponsor is living in Quebec or you plan on living in Quebec when your application is approved, the IRCC will direct you to apply for a CSQ from MIDI once they've completed processing your federal application. See the section on Quebec for more information.

Provincial Nomination Programs

Canada has a number of Provincial Nomination Programs (PNPs) that allow provinces to sponsor people for permanent residence status. These programs change frequently. Some PNPs have online applications separate from the IRCC website, some are integrated into Express Entry, and others require a paper application.

Many are designed to allow temporary residents, like students and temporary workers, to stay permanently. If you have ties to a certain province or territory, you should see if you qualify for a PNP.

Others are designed to meet specific skill shortages. These skill lists change regularly, so if you don't qualify now you may qualify in the future.

All PNPs require you to state your intent to settle permanently in whichever province sponsors your immigration into Canada. You must still meet all of the requirements for federal immigration, in addition to the requirements of the PNP you are applying for.

The number of admissions through the PNPs has grown each year since EE has switched from paper to an online system. It is set to accept over 71k permanent residents in 2021. When PNP was introduced in 1996, only 233 people were accepted through the programs.

Canadian graduates

Provinces can nominate candidates outside of the Express Entry system, typically for people who do not meet EE requirements. Outside of the EE system, candidates must first get a provincial nomination. Once you have the nomination certificate, you can apply for immigration through the federal government using the paper application. You can find all the forms on the IRCC website. The paper immigration application has a much longer processing time.

If you have a degree from a Canadian university and have a valid job offer from an approved company, you likely qualify for PNP for your province.

If you've gotten your Master's degree or PhD in Canada, you'll likely qualify for PNP in your province and may even get an open work permit while your application to become a permanent resident is processed.

Business Class Immigration

Running a business in Canada can provide a pathway to PR status. If you're already an entrepreneur, you can bring your business to Canada. If you have a startup idea, you can build your business in Canada. You can even buy or invest in an established business.

Entrepreneur PNP

If you have financial capital and business experience, there are several programs set up that would allow you to immigrate to Canada and invest in the economy. Each province and territory has their own PNP with entrepreneur streams to get you started on the pathway to residency. Some PNPs will grant you permanent residency status before you move, and others will sponsor permanent residency only after you've been successfully operating your new business in Canada for a specific amount of time.

These programs vary slightly between each province, but generally all require that you become an active partner in a new or existing business located within that province. They require that you prove your net worth, demonstrate the ability to contribute a certain amount of equity into a business, and to make a sizeable deposit to that province that will be held by the government for a specific amount of time or until your business plan has been fully executed.

Most of the PNPs that are open to business investors have caps and only accept a certain number of applicants per year. Depending on which province you're interested in living in, you may need to wait in order to even apply. Since the PNPs aim to address specific economic needs, the requirements and selection criteria may change at any time.

You'll need to submit a viable business plan along with your application and would meet with a government representative to discuss your strategy. Priority is given to applicants that are most qualified and thought to have the greatest potential to establish themselves in that province and make the biggest contribution to the economy. Meeting the technical requirements does not guarantee your acceptance into the program.

The purpose of these programs is to contribute to the economy and to create jobs, so your business plan would need to address the creation of new full-time jobs for Canadians, not just for yourself or family members.

In addition to whichever requirements exist for each PNP, you and any accompanying family members would need to pass a medical exam and prove that you would not be an excessive burden on the health and social services offered by the government. You'd also have to prove proficiency in English and/or French and, of course, be considered admissible to Canada.

Move your start-up to Canada

Running a startup? Canada is looking to hold its own against Silicon Valley, so they're building an excellent network to nurture startups and attract top talent. If approved, you'd be able to move to Canada as a permanent resident through the Start-Up Business Class immigration stream.

Unlike most other immigration programs, this one does not necessarily favor younger applicants. Up to five people can move to Canada under the startup visa. You'll need to take a language test to prove your proficiency in English and/or French.

You need to prove you have funds to support yourself and your family. The requirements are quite reasonable and if you're moving to a city, you'll want to have access to more funds than that if you don't have some sort of income coming in.

You'll need support from a designated VC fund, angel investor, or business incubator.

Each person coming on a startup visa needs to have at least 10% of the votes and collectively, the startup applicants and designated organization need to have a majority stake.

Requirements
- Guaranteed minimum investment from a designated organization
- Own at least 10% of your business
- Verified voting rights that, along with any other applicant and designated organization, is equal to or greater than 50%
- Have completed at least a year of post-secondary education
- Ability to communicate in English or French
- Do not intend to live in the province of Quebec
- Have the minimal amount of savings to support yourself (about $12,000 and additional $2,000 per family member that would immigrate with you)

Investment
While you can obtain investments from just about anyone, you'll need to secure minimal support from at least one of the three types of designated organizations:
1. Venture capital fund: C$200k minimum investment
2. Angel investor group: C$75k minimum investment
3. Business incubator program: no investment required

Within each of these categories, there are a limited number of organizations that qualify within each option. Check the list of designated organizations provided by the IRCC in order to find the most up to date list.

Each organization has their own set of criteria in place to evaluate the potential of your business plan. You'd be responsible for establishing contact and pitching your idea in an effort to obtain their support.

If one of the organizations decides that they would like to invest in your business, you'd also be responsible for getting a Letter of Support to submit as part of your immigration application. The organization will also need to submit a Commitment Certificate directly to the IRCC to verify their support. This certificate would outline the agreement between you and the organization in regards to the business venture.

If the only way you can reach the minimum investment amount is through support from multiple organizations, you'll be considered to be in syndication. In that case, you'll need to provide letters of support from each organization. If any one of the organizations is a venture capital firm, then you will need to meet the minimum investment amount of C$200k, even if all of the other groups pledging support are angel investors.

All commitments are subject to a peer review process.

Ownership

You don't have to be the sole proprietor of your business in order to be eligible for the visa. You, along with up to four other owners, can apply for the visa. Once your investment is secured, each owner would submit their own application for the start-up visa. Each owner must retain at least 10% of the voting rights for the business in order to qualify for the start-up visa. Additionally, all owners, together with all investors, must hold more than 50% of all voting rights for the business.

If your business is owned by more than just yourself, the investor commitment can be conditional. That would mean that their promise of investment would only be guaranteed if whichever person (or people) was identified as "essential." In that situation, the investment would only be given if the essential applicant was approved for immigration. If that person was rejected for the visa, then all other owners would also be rejected.

Self-employed

If you're a successful author, musician, athlete, or the like, you can become a Canadian permanent resident through the self-employment visa program. You need to be working in cultural activities or athletics at a world-class level.

This is also the program farmers can immigrate through, but at the moment that program is paused.

They take your age, language skills, education, experience, and adaptability into account, on a points system. You and your family members must have a medical exam and get police certificates. You must also show that you have enough money to support yourself and your family after you get to Canada.

Part Five: Express Entry

Immigrating to Canada feels sort of like being a contestant on a dating show. You want to highlight your best qualities so they'll choose you and you can live happily ever after. Only every challenge is incredibly boring and involves calling your boss from six years ago to get paperwork or filling out a thousand tiny boxes online.

How EE works

Like any good reality tv show, they need to stretch it out to fill a whole season, so the process can feel a little convoluted. I'll explain the whole process briefly here and then walk you through it in more detail. There are a lot of details, but none of them are difficult.

First, find out if you meet the basic eligibility requirements to apply by filling out a short questionnaire on the IRCC website.

Assuming you're eligible, you'll create an Express Entry profile, detailing your skills, work experience, language abilities, education, along with everything you've done in your life and every country you've visited in the past ten years. If you meet the basic criteria, you'll be accepted into the candidate pool. Your profile is your expression of interest (EOI) in immigrating to Canada.

You will be assigned a comprehensive ranking system (CRS) score based on the information you provided in your profile. Perhaps you took a quiz online or calculated your CRS points yourself to estimate your score, but this is your official score.

If you don't already have a qualifying job offer, you can register with the job bank. Theoretically this connects employees to employers. If you get a job offer through the job bank, you can get a work permit in as little as two weeks and will move right to the next step, without languishing in the candidate pool. You're encouraged to look for a job while you're in the pool and there's no reason to limit yourself to postings in the job bank.

If you're selected from the pool, you receive an invitation to apply (ITA). You have 90 days to add more information to your profile and submit it as your application for permanent residence.

Gathering paperwork and getting it translated can be a lengthy process, so it's best to begin getting your paperwork ready before you have your ITA. If you do not submit your application within 90 days and you don't respond to the ITA, your profile is removed from the system and you have to start over again.

If you can't get your documents in time, you can decline the ITA and you will be placed back in the candidate pool, so you theoretically could receive a second ITA.

Once your application is submitted, you wait. The IRCC may request additional information or schedule an interview. You'll get occasional email updates to let you know where your application is in the process.

The process generally takes about six months from when you submit your complete application to when you get final approval to move. Some people have their application processed in weeks, especially if you are already living and working in Canada. If you're not in Canada, this is a great time to visit Canada and start getting ready to move. Just remember that you haven't been approved yet and your application could still hit a snag.

Once you're approved, you get documents allowing you to travel to the border and declaring yourself a landed immigrant. You have a year from the date of your medical exam to immigrate. If you don't move before your medical exam expires, you will have to start the process over again from the beginning.

If you don't get an ITA, your profile expires after a year. You can make a new profile and try again.

Basic requirements

- You must be admissible to Canada
- You'll need to prove that you are fluent in English or French by taking a language test, even if you are a native speaker
- You'll need to demonstrate that you are in relatively good health
- You have at least a year of work experience as a manager, professional, or skilled trades person
- You can provide all of the necessary documentation
- You intent to live in any province or territory except Québec, unless you have a CSQ

Who can come with you?

You'll need to include personal details for all the members of your family as part of your own application, even if they are not moving with you. Assuming you are invited to immigrate, your spouse or common law partner and dependent children would automatically be invited along with you.

Express Entry

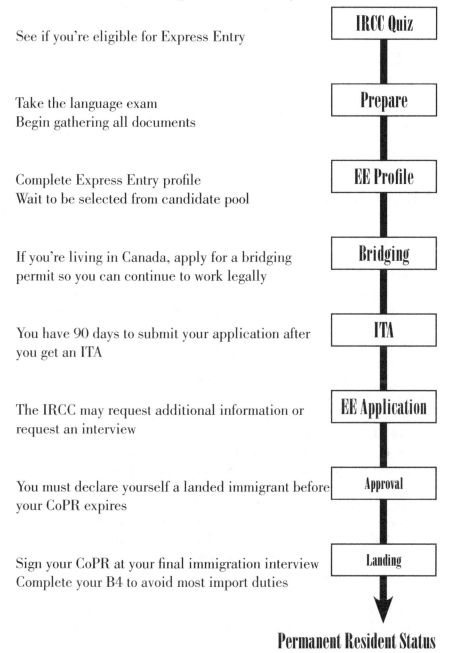

See if you're eligible for Express Entry — **IRCC Quiz**

Take the language exam
Begin gathering all documents — **Prepare**

Complete Express Entry profile
Wait to be selected from candidate pool — **EE Profile**

If you're living in Canada, apply for a bridging
permit so you can continue to work legally — **Bridging**

You have 90 days to submit your application after
you get an ITA — **ITA**

The IRCC may request additional information or
request an interview — **EE Application**

You must declare yourself a landed immigrant before
your CoPR expires — **Approval**

Sign your CoPR at your final immigration interview
Complete your B4 to avoid most import duties — **Landing**

Permanent Resident Status

All dependents need to have a medical examination, even if they are not accompanying you. If any of your children are between the ages of 18 and 22, they will also need to provide a police certificate, even if they are not coming with you.

Is EE new?

If you're the sort of person who talks about immigration systems over beers, you might have heard that Express Entry is a new program. That's not strictly true. It just brings the Federal Skilled Worker, Federal Skilled Trades, Canadian Experience, and the Provincial Nominee Programs online. It makes the process a lot faster and more flexible.

The Comprehensive Ranking System

The Comprehensive Ranking System (CRS) is EE's points system. It aims to assess your likelihood of adapting to life in Canada and doing well there, as well as your ability to improve the Canadian economy. Scores range from 0 to 1,200.

Unfortunately for those of us over the age of 29, the Canadian Express Entry program is specifically designed for young professionals. The younger you are, the less work experience you need to have in order to qualify.

After the age of 35, your chances of being accepted into the Express Entry program decline significantly. It's nearly impossible to get an ITA if you're over 45 unless you have a valid job offer or a provincial nomination. The IRCC even adjusted the number of points a job offer gets you in order to reduce the number of older workers who were being given ITAs.

Your CRS is based on you and your partner, if you're married or in a common law relationship. If your partner is not coming with you to Canada, you can calculate your CRS as if you were single. You can also calculate your points as if you were single if your partner is already a Canadian citizen or permanent resident.

Theoretically, an invitation to apply is offered to people who:
- Are among the top ranked in the Express Entry pool
- Are nominated by a province or territory
- Have a qualifying job offer

You'll know your score and the scores for the most recent batch of prospective immigrants to be invited to apply, but you won't know where you rank in the current pool.

Needing to be top ranked seems a little intimidating. Living in New York City made me feel like a loser because I hadn't made our first million by the age of 30. In fact, I still haven't made my first million. I didn't get a perfect score on the SATs. I didn't graduate top in my class, ever, except that one year when I was the only student in my grade. I'm not rabidly pursued by headhunters. When I tried to get a mortgage every bank turned me down. No one is really sure what I do for a living. Thankfully, the IRCC is less judgmental than your average New Yorker.

How many points do I need?

There is no official minimum score to get an ITA – and no number of points guarantees an invitation. Based on who's been invited to apply so far, if you have a score of 450 or higher, you'll get an ITA right away. My score was 451 and I got an ITA within a week.

You only need to get 67 points in order to enter the pool. People with scores below 450 get ITAs every year. People in the FSTC have gotten ITAs with scores as low as 199.

The IRCC publishes the scores for each EE class after every draw. Once you calculate your score – using either an online score calculator, the CRS matrix, or actually creating a profile – you can decide if it's worth getting your paperwork ready in hopes of getting an ITA.

Speaking French and your CRS score

In addition to getting points for your language ability, being bilingual in Canada's official languages boosts your chances of getting provincial nomination.

If you are fluent in French, have an advanced degree, and can demonstrate three or more years of professional experience, then you might qualify for the Ontario Immigrant Nominee Program (OINP).

OINP seeks specifically to bring French speakers into the predominantly English-speaking province. There's no way to apply directly to this program, instead just submit your Express Entry profile and enter that you intend to live in Ontario. Once your profile is reviewed, you'd receive a notification letting you know that you qualify for the OINP program along with instructions for how to continue.

This is great if you wouldn't otherwise score high enough to get an ITA. If you already have a CRS score high enough to get you an ITA, PNP is an unnecessary layer of paperwork and fees.

Ways to increase your CRS score
- Get a qualifying job offer
- Increase your English language exam score

- Learn French
- Increase your work experience
- Get more educational training, especially from a Canadian university
- Work in Canada under a work permit or working holiday
- Get provincial nomination
- If you have a spouse, have them increase their language proficiency or education level
- Talk your sibling into moving to Canada

The best way to increase your score is to find a Canadian employer willing to offer you a job or get a provincial nomination. Almost everyone with a low personal CRS score who has been invited to apply has had a provincial nomination.

Things that don't increase your score

The IRCC is not interested in your current salary or your remote job. The only thing you need to prove is that you meet the basic funds requirement. If you have a qualifying job offer they don't even look at your finances. Having an income source, such as remote work, rental properties, or annuities, does not get you points.

If you're wealthy or an entrepreneur and have a low CRS score, considerer immigrating through one of the business class programs.

You might think that owning a home in Canada would count for something. It doesn't.

Can an immigration attorney increase your score?

No. Your Express Entry points are based on your personal factors. An immigration attorney or consultant can't increase your score unless you initially filled the forms out incorrectly and you weren't allocated the correct number of points as a result or if they're committing fraud. Immigration attorneys occasionally make the news for fake job offers and other tricks to increase CRS points.

If your immigration consultant boosts your score illegally and is caught, you (and your family) can be deported.

Your NOC code

Canada uses the National Occupation Classification (NOC) code system to determine what counts as skilled work for EE. You'll need work experience in an NOC that falls within skill level 0, A, or B.

If you manage a team, regardless of whether that team works in an office, restaurant, or on a boat, you likely fit into class 0. If you sit at a desk all day and have a degree, you're probably in class A. If you went to vocational school, did an apprenticeship, or have a degree from a trade school, you're probably in class B.

You'll need to find the NOC code that matches the types of job(s) you worked at for at least 12 months in order to apply to Express Entry. The IRCC has put some effort into categorizing some of the more popular job types, but chances are that you'll need to do some research to find the right NOC code. Start broad and look for the most appropriate unit group. The NOC job title might not match up exactly with your official title, but so long as its close and your employer will vouch for you, it should be okay.

If you worked two different types of jobs that are both in Skill Level 0, A, or B categories, you can still apply so long as it adds up to at least 12 months of full time work over the last 10 years.

This can still apply to you if you've been self-employed, but you'll need to provide proof of income and verification letters from clients, vendors, or buyers that document your experience. I didn't have any trouble with this and it was nice to have an excuse to get lunch with former clients.

If a company you worked for or a former client has gone out of business, don't worry. If you hoard paperwork, you can provide old documents to verify your work. If you're still in touch with former co-workers, they can write a letter for you. You can also include proof that the business has dissolved. I've worked for a lot of small businesses and startups, so I provided a lot of non-standard documents and the IRCC accepted these without issue.

Express Entry Classes

The Federal Skilled Worker Program

The Federal Skilled Worker Program (FSWP) program is one of the easiest ways a non-Canadian can immigrate as a permanent resident. The FSWP does not require that you have a job offer or any connection to Canada.

The program looks for qualified people that will contribute to the culture and economy of Canada. This program primarily assesses your age, work history, education, and language skills. If you are under 35, have professional experience, have an advanced degree, and are fluent in English or French, chances are you'll be invited into the FSWP program.

Basic requirements

- You've worked in an applicable NOC field full-time (30+ hours a week) for at least 12 months in the last 10 years. Or, you've worked the equivalent in part time hours, such as 15 hours a week for 24 months
- You can prove that you held at least one job in an applicable NOC field for at least 12 continuous months
- You can provide letters from all employers that you've worked for over the last 10 years verifying that you worked there along with your primary duties, length of employment, title, salary, benefits, hours, and NOC code (you'll still need letters for jobs that aren't related to the NOC field)
- You'll need to have your academic diplomas evaluated by a IRCC approved third party such as World Education Services (WES) in order to prove that they are equivalent to Canadian degrees
- If you don't have a qualifying job offer, you must have at least C$12,500. You'll need more, depending on how many family members you have. The IRCC assumes you'll continue supporting your family, even if they don't come with you to Canada. If your partner is on your application, their funds can be included in this. Only accessible funds count towards this amount, so you can't include any retirement accounts.

Federal Skilled Trades

The Federal Skilled Trades Class (FSTC) program brings tradespeople to Canada. The FSTC requires that you have a valid job offer in Canada or are already certified to work in your trade within the country of Canada.

Certification exams are offered by governing bodies in each province and sometimes require related work experience within that province. You will likely have to appear in person to have your qualifications assessed by an employer in Canada in order for a valid job offer in your trade. If you don't already have a certificate of qualification, you can still apply if you can convince the IRCC that you would be eligible to obtain any necessary certifications required for your trade job.

FSTC applicants are often already be working in Canada as a temporary foreign worker with a work permit. Only 3,000 people can apply under this program each year and some of the individual NOC titles have caps of 100 applicants per year.

People applying under this program are not required to have advanced degrees; though having one will help to increase your score.

Work experience

To qualify under the FSTC program you'll need to have at least two years of full time work experience in the past five years in one of these types of jobs:

- Major Group 72, industrial, electrical and construction trades,
- Major Group 73, maintenance and equipment operation trades,
- Major Group 82, supervisors and technical jobs in natural resources, agriculture and related production,
- Major Group 92, processing, manufacturing and utilities supervisors and central control operators,
- Minor Group 632, chefs and cooks, and
- Minor Group 633, butchers and bakers.

The IRCC has a NOC matrix that provides a good overview of the major job types that would qualify for this immigration program.

Canadian Experience Class

If you've worked in Canada legally for a year or more, on an open work permit through your partner, working holiday visa, post-graduation work permit, or NAFTA work permit, you may qualify to become a permanent resident through Express Entry.

It makes sense that Canada would want to make it easy for people who are currently living and working in Canada to stay. If you're already living here -- or have lived here in the past -- you've already demonstrated your ability to thrive in Canada.

Not every job qualifies you for Express Entry's Canadian Experience Class (EE CEC) and work done on a student visa doesn't count. Neither does working remotely for a Canadian company. You'll need to provide proof that you were (or are) authorized to work in Canada and you filed your taxes.

Your work also needs to have been in a qualifying profession. This is determined by the NOC code system. Qualifying jobs are:

- Skill Level 0: Management – almost any type of job that includes manager or supervisor in the title
- Skill Level A: Professional – most office jobs
- Skill Level B: Technical – these jobs often require an Associate's degree or apprenticeship of some kind

Provincial Nominee Programs

Because different regions of Canada have different economies and cultures, these programs allow Canadian provinces and territories to select potential immigrants based on their needs. This is the purpose of Provincial Nominee Programs (PNP). Some of these programs are integrated into EE, which is what I'm talking about here.

The requirements of these programs change regularly. If you're worried that your CRS score is too low to get an ITA, check into the current PNPs and see if you qualify for any of them. Some PNPs will choose candidates that qualify from the pool, others require a separate application first.

If your CRS score is low, but you have skills or experience that a particular province needs, you may get a provincial nomination. Provincial nomination will add 600 points to your CRS score.

They'll also add to the amount of time it will take to process your application and come with their own paperwork and fees.

Not everyone who gets a provincial nomination accepts it. If you believe you can get an ITA without PNP, you may decide it's not worth the hassle and expense of the PNP process.

A step-by-step guide to EE

The first step of Express Entry is using the Come to Canada tool on the IRCC website. They'll give you a Personal Reference Code that saves your information for 30 days.

The next step is to create your Express Entry profile, using your Personal Reference Code.

You know those online job applications that have you upload your resume and then make you type it all out, one line at a time? That's what the Express Entry profile is like, only it wants to know a lot more about you and your family. It took some time for me to find start and end dates for:

- Every job I've ever had,
- Every place I've ever lived,
- Every school I've ever attended, and
- Every country I've ever visited.

Mercifully, you can save your profile and log back in later. You have 60 days to complete your profile, otherwise you'll have to start over again.

When you create your account, you'll get a MyCIC number. Save that information or you'll have a heck of a time trying to log back in.

Gmail was automatically sorting notifications from the IRCC to the trash folder, so I set up a filter rule to make sure emails from donotreply@cic.

gc.ca would be marked as important and not vanish into my spam folder. You might want to do something like this for your own email account to make sure you don't miss any updates or requests for additional information from the IRCC.

Regardless, it's probably a good idea to login to your IRCC account occasionally to make sure you haven't missed any important notifications.

Things you'll need

You can't create a profile without:

- A passport or another national identity document
- Language test results
- The ability to scan and upload documents
- A credit card to pay the fees

Optional paperwork

- Education Credential Assessment (required for you and/or your spouse if either of you are trying to get points for academic degrees)
- Written job offer
- Provincial nomination

While this is the only paperwork you need to have in order to create your profile, I highly recommend you begin gathering all the paperwork you'll need before you even submit your profile. I got an ITA right away and the paperwork took so long to gather that I probably would have run out of time had I not had everything ready to go when I submitted my profile.

Work history

Calling this your work history is a bit of a misnomer. This is not intended to be a resume or CV like you'd submit in a job application, this is a timeline of everything you've done as an adult.

There's no clear way to account for time spent being unemployed, traveling, or providing care for a relative. The engineers who designed this must have had a very clear life path. I improvised. You cannot have any gaps in time, so write out what you were doing and fill in any blank fields with N/A.

I've done a lot of contract and freelance work, so it wasn't easy to complete the work history section. I did my best to accurately portray my work experience in their system. Given the number of graphic designers who've been invited to apply, they appear to be okay with that.

At this stage, you don't need to provide any documentation to prove your work history. However, if the documents in your application don't match what you put here, your application can be rejected.

Addresses

Perhaps you're the type of person who's lived in one place your whole life. The IRCC is ready for that.

I'm not one of those people.

Hopefully they've fixed this, but when I submitted my profile, they didn't allow letters or special characters in house or apartment numbers. I've had a few previous addresses that contained fractions or letters, which were rejected when I tried to enter them. I left out the offending characters and my application was accepted, so I wouldn't worry too much about this.

The address of my childhood home has changed several times, although it's the same house in the same location. My family ignored this and our friendly mailman continued to deliver our mail, regardless of which address it was sent to, but I wasn't sure how the IRCC would respond to this confusing situation. I simply used the original address and they never asked for clarification.

Language test results

Everyone needs to take a language test, even if English is the only language you speak. It seems silly, but rules are rules.

It sounds even more ridiculous that they tell native English speakers to study before the test. This is good advice. Like any standardized test, it feels more like a test of your test taking skills than on your language abilities. There are plenty of native English speakers who don't get a perfect score, but you'll certainly pass. You can take practice tests online if you'd like to get a better idea of what you're in for.

I took the general training module test through IELTS (International English Language Testing System). They have testing locations throughout the world, but if you don't live near a major city, then be prepared to travel. The testing slots fill up fast, so schedule your test sooner rather than later. You will need a valid passport when you arrive for the test in order to be admitted into the testing room.

The test itself feels a lot like the SATs. You leave all of your personal belongings in a separate room, including your wallet and cell phone, then you're given a pencil to take a hand written test. The test is made up of four different parts: listening, reading, writing, and speaking. This will involve listening to an audio recording of a subject matter and answering questions about what you heard, reading a short story then answering questions about what you read, writing essays about two different topics, and finally talking to a test facilitator for about 30 minutes on an assigned subject. Expect to spend about six hours getting quizzed in how well you speak, write, and understand English.

The test is not necessarily difficult, but it is time consuming and somewhat stressful, especially if you aren't used to writing things out by hand for several hours straight or needing to ask permission to go to the bathroom. The whole experience felt a lot like being back in high school.

The test results will be mailed to you about two weeks after you complete the test. They'll include a code that you'll need to enter into your EE profile.

Education Credential Assessment

Canadian employers recognize degrees from abroad, but the IRCC doesn't. You'll need to get your credentials assessed by an approved company if you're applying under the skilled worker class.

Applicants under the skilled trades or Canadian experience class don't necessarily need an Education Credential Assessment (ECA), but you won't get points for your education without it. If you need the points, it's worth the hassle.

If you aren't sure how your foreign training will be recognized in Cnaada, the World Education Services (WES) has an online tool that will tell you what your degree is equivalent to for free. You will, of course, still have to send them the documents and pay the fee for this to count toward your CRS.

I got a "Course-by-Course" evaluation from WES. It took about six weeks between when I submitted everything to when I received the official letters authenticating my degrees from US colleges. Those six weeks don't include the three or more weeks of waiting beforehand for each school to mail transcripts directly to WES.

WES will ask for several different documents for each degree that you are seeking an ECA for:

- Photocopy of your actual diploma or graduation certificate
- Academic transcripts sent directly to WES from your school (usually an additional $25-$50 each, unless they now use the Parchment system)
- A legal document verifying any name change if the name on your diploma or transcripts does not match your current legal name (such as a marriage certificate or divorce order)

Don't assume you can just mail a transcript request form and actually get one. Unexpected bureaucracy can add significantly to how long your paperwork will take to get ready. My undergraduate registrar insisted I had an outstanding debt, so they wouldn't send the transcript, but the bursar had no record of the debt, so they wouldn't let me pay it. Clearing up this $20 dispute took months.

If you didn't keep a copy of your diploma, you'll have to pay your school for them to send you a new one (which cost me $50 per diploma).

The ECA that WES provides is valid for five years.

Registering on the Canada Job Bank

After you submit your profile, you can register with the job bank. This used to be mandatory, but now it's optional.

Theoretically, employers can check out your resumes that you've posted to the job bank and offer you an interview at their company, but the job postings I saw weren't relevant to my field and the inquiries I got from employers were seemingly random.

However, if you were to find a job through the job bank you can get a work permit in as little as two weeks and you'll probably get an ITA in the next round of invitations.

Waiting in the pool for an ITA

Hopefully at this point you'll get an email letting you know you have a top secret message in your MyCIC account to let you know you've been placed in the Express Entry pool. You'll also be told your official CRS score.

Don't just sit back and relax. Continue gathering your paperwork and looking for work. If anything you've put in your profile changes, you'll need to update your profile.

Once the IRCC has a chance to review your Express Entry profile and determines that you meet the criteria to immigrate, you'll receive an invitation to apply (ITA) for permanent resident status. I received my ITA about a week after I submitted my profile.

If one of your kids turns 22 while you're waiting for an ITA, they're no longer considered a dependent and would require their own application. Once you receive an ITA and your application is submitted, their (and your) age is considered to be "locked in," but until then they can age out of dependent status and you can lose points for your age.

Preparing your application

Once you get your ITA, you have 90 days to submit your complete application. If your documents don't support the number of CRS points initially awarded or you're deemed inadmissible, your application will be denied.

If you can't get the paperwork together in time, you can decline the ITA and you'll be placed back in the pool. If you're eligible for multiple programs, you may be invited to apply again.

If you don't decline the ITA or submit an application within 90 days, you'll be removed from the pool. You'll have to start over if you'd like to be invited to apply again.

Paperwork you'll need

- Police certificate (for you and any adult family members)
- Language test results (for you and an accompanying partner)
- Educational credential assessment (if you want points for education)
- Medical exam (for you and any family members)
- Proof of funds (if you don't have a valid job offer and are not already legally living in Canada)
- Verification of your work history
- Proof of relationship status, if applicable:
  - Marriage certificate
  - Divorce certificate
  - Death certificate if you are a widow
  - Evidence of a common law relationship
- Proof of parental status, if applicable:
  - Birth certificates for any dependent children
  - Adoption certificates for any adopted dependents

Other information to gather

- All addresses you've ever lived at
- All international travel within the past 10 years
- Personal information about all immediate family members, even if they will not be immigrating (such as full names, addresses, and date of birth)

Police certificates

You and any family members who are 18 or older will need police certificates for any country you've lived in for at least six consecutive months for the past ten years or since you (or they) turned 18. They're valid for six months for the country you're currently living in. For other countries it can date from any time after you left, even if it has an expiration date that's passed.

You should request this very early in the process, since many countries are slow to provide this. The IRCC will accept proof that you've requested this so you can submit your profile before the deadline, but your application can't be approved without it.

Some countries require a consent form before issuing a police certificate. If you need a police certificate from one of these countries, you submit the consent form to the IRCC in place of the police certificate and the IRCC will then request a police certificate from that country on your behalf.

The FBI doesn't provide any status updates or even proof that they received your request. You need to be fingerprinted by your local police department before you can submit the request to the FBI. Since I was living in NYC, I spent an afternoon at the NYPD headquarters getting this part done. It took about two hours and wasn't nearly as unpleasant as I expected it to be.

Medical exam

You can't just go to any doctor; you need to see a panel physician for your medical exam, and there aren't a lot of them located in each country. Be sure to mention you need an Express Entry medical exam when you make an appointment. Chances are the office will know exactly what you're talking about and exactly what they need to give you. If they don't, try a different panel physician in your area.

The IRCC recommends you wait until you get your ITA before scheduling your medical exam. Your exam results are only valid for 12 months and need to have at least six months remaining when you submit your application. If the medical exam is valid for less than six months, you'll have to get another exam done. I scheduled my appointment as soon as I received my ITA.

The date that you get your medical exam is extremely important because the date your permanent resident visa expires is based on this. Your PR visa is the paperwork allowing you to become a permanent resident.

When you go to your appointment, bring two passport photos, your MyCIC number application number, and your passport.

You will need to give a general medical history, get blood work and a chest x-ray. My x-ray tech seemed very excited to tell me that I didn't have TB.

It seems like the blood work is to rule out HIV and syphilis. You won't automatically be deemed inadmissible if your blood work comes back positive. However, once the IRCC has gotten your test results you have 60 days to withdraw your application or they will notify your partner of your status. If you'd like to continue with EE, you'll want to voluntarily disclose your status to your partner, if you haven't already.

The doctor will submit your medical exam results directly to the IRCC and likely won't give you any actual information to you.

The doctor may give you a sealed letter that you will need to hold onto. In theory, the immigration office might ask to see this letter when you arrive at the port of entry to declare yourself a landed immigrant I wasn't asked to show mine, but you'll want to hold onto this in case you are asked for it.

A few weeks after the medical exam, you'll receive an update on your IRCC page letting you know if you passed the medical exam.

The cost of the immigration medical exam will not be covered by your health insurance.

Proof of funds

The proof of funds required starts at C$12,669 for a single person and increases based on the number of people in your immediate family, regardless of whether or not they're immigrating with you.

- If you don't need to show proof of funds if you:
  have a qualifying job offer and a valid work permit, or
- are applying through the Canadian Experience Class.

The IRCC wants to make sure you have some money to set up a home and cover your living expenses when you first arrive in the country. It's reasonable to assume you might be to be unemployed for a period of time while you find a job. Simply moving can be quite expensive.

If you are currently living in Canada, but aren't applying through the Canadian Experience Class or don't have a valid work permit, you still need to provide proof of funds.

Perhaps you work remotely and will keep your current job, have another income source like rental properties, or have a job offer that doesn't qualify for points through Express Entry. The IRCC will not take these into consideration.

If you plan to immigrate with your spouse, cash in either of your bank accounts will count towards the total amount of funds you'll need to document.

Since they want to make sure you haven't borrowed this money, you'll need to prove that you have had this money in your personal accounts for several months before applying.

You will need to get an official letter from your bank printed on letterhead that includes:

- Your name
- Bank address, telephone, and email address
- Account numbers
- Total funds in each account
- Date each account was open
- Current balance of accounts
- Average balance of each account for the past six months

Getting proof of funds ended up being more difficult than it should have been, partly because I had accounts at more than one bank. Bank officers really wanted to give me the information that the United States immigration process requires, rather than what I needed for Canadian immigration.

If your bank refuses to provide a letter with the information the IRCC requires, try to get them to put in writing that they cannot comply with your request. You can provide this along with several months of bank statements.

Verification of your work history

If you're applying as a skilled worker, you will need to prove that you're actually a skilled worker. Makes sense, right? This is actually one of the hardest things to put together for the application, since you have to account for the last ten years of your work history. This means you'll need to reach out to every employer you've worked for in the past decade, even if it didn't end well.

Canadian Experience Class

If you're applying through the Canadian Experience Class, then you're in luck because you only have to account for whichever jobs you've worked in Canada. Since you only need a single year of qualifying work experience in Canada, this probably means only having to get a letter from a single employer. It won't hurt to account for however many years of qualifying experience you have in Canada.

If you're applying through this program, you'll also need to provide your most recent work permit, T4 tax information slips, and Notice of Assessments.

Proof of employment history

Proving your work experience is rarely as simple as it would seem. Even people who've worked for one company for the past ten years have probably held different job titles or even worked for different divisions. Who should write the letter? What should it contain?

Many of us have gaps in our employment history, have worked for our own companies, or were freelance workers. Plenty of companies go out of business each year. There are a lot of questions that come up when talking about how to verify your employment experience.

Thankfully, while the IRCC website doesn't give the clear instructions for non-traditional employees that we might like, these things won't disqualify you from moving to Canada as a skilled worker using Express Entry.

Your work verification letter should be written by either a member of your company human resources department or your supervisor.

The letter should be written on company letterhead and a business card for the person writing the letter should be attached. The author of the letter should sign it and include their full name and title. If your company has an official seal, be sure to get the letter stamped.

If you've had multiple positions within the same company, you can either have separate letters for each position or include the relevant information (title, responsibilities, and dates) for each position you've held included in the same letter.

Your employer is probably used to being asked for character references. While the IRCC will be happy to know you're a good employee and an upstanding citizen, they're more interested in your job duties.

You'll need to get an official letter from each employer on company letterhead that includes:

- Your legal name as it appears on your Express Entry profile and identity documents
- Company's address, telephone, and email address
- The full name, job title, and contact information for the person writing the letter
- Your official job title and the corresponding NOC code
- Your hire date and either that you are still employed there or the date you stopped working there
- The average number of hours worked per week
- Your salary, hourly rate, or other payment information
- Benefits included in your salary or in addition to your salary
- A detailed description of your responsibilities

I wrote a draft of what I needed each company to verify, then sent it out to the employer with a request that they review and return it on company letterhead. For larger companies, this will probably need to go through the HR department. Since you don't have much control over how fast this part goes, get started on it soon so you're not stuck waiting around for it at the end.

For jobs that align to the NOC you're applying under, make sure the responsibilities of the job match the NOC description. Just like you may tailor your resume for a specific job posting, you can tailor your job description to ensure that it matches your NOC code. The person assessing your application may not be familiar with the jargon of your field, so make sure it's easy for them to see that there's a match between your role and the NOC code you're applying under.

Don't just copy/paste the NOC code description into the letter. You need to provide a description of your work responsibilities that is customized to your position that incorporates key phrases and terms from the NOC code. Your official job title is less important than the description of your role.

This part of your application will be thoroughly reviewed so make sure you demonstrate that you are qualified to immigrate as a skilled worker.

What work needs to be documented?

It's very important to document the previous three years of work experience. Any other work experience related to the NOC code you're applying under should also be documented to the best of your ability.

Insufficient proof of your work history can get your Express Entry application rejected. The meaning of 'sufficient' proof is subjective. It's up to the person assessing your application to decide how much is enough to decide you should get PR.

If you're the accompanying spouse, you should still provide documentation for any relevant work history. However, a poorly documented work history of a spouse is less likely to lead to your application being delayed or rejected.

Do you need to spend weeks tracking down a supervisor from that defunct company you worked for seven years ago in a completely unrelated job? Probably not. However, it doesn't hurt to play it safe and provide some verification, like old pay stubs, contracts, or tax forms.

Self employment

The IRCC recognizes that many people today work for their own companies and do freelance work. This won't hold you back from immigrating through Express Entry.

Provide a letter explaining that you were self employed and providing a detailed description of the services you provide(d). If your services changed over time, include this information.

Include reference letters from clients to verify this information. These reference letters should follow the same format as the standard letters above.

You can include any additional documentation, such as:
- Client contracts
- Proof of payment from clients or vendors
- Business registration paperwork
- Tax filings
- Screenshots of your website or promotional materials

What if you can't get a letter?

What happens if you can't get a work verification letter? Or if your company will not include all of the required information in the letter? You simply need to provide additional documents to ensure the people assessing your application will be able to feel you have demonstrated your work history.

Some companies have policies forbidding them from providing salary information or other details in a letter, meaning they can't provide you the letter the IRCC is asking for. You can use additional documentation to fill in the gaps, like your original contract, tax forms, or cancelled cheques.

The IRCC has made it very clear that it is the applicant's responsibility to demonstrate their work history to the satisfaction of the person assessing your application. The less clear your work history is, the more likely your application is to be delayed while you provide additional documentation or denied outright.

Provide additional documentation

I had one former employer provide me with a letter that lacked the required information. I provided their letter with additional documents to fill in the gaps and provide the information the IRCC is looking for. If you have gaps in your documents, see if you can dig up:

- The original job posting
- Your original offer letter
- Employment contracts
- Printouts from the company intranet showing your role
- Emails confirming your role
- Tax forms (W-2, 1099, T4)
- Paystubs
- Bank statements (showing your salary being deposited)
- Old proof of employment letters
- Old reference letters
- Company newsletters that mention you and your work
- Pictures of you at work
- Letters from coworkers or clients

If a company has gone out of business, you can contact your former supervisor or another former company executive to write a letter stating that the company is no longer active and verifying your employment. It's advisable to pair this with additional documents if you have them.

If you are unable to provide any letter at all, write a letter of your own explaining why. Provide any evidence you can to demonstrate your work history and corroborate your explanation, such as:

- Newspaper articles showing that the company has shut down
- Obituary for your former supervisor

- Screenshots from the company website showing that they are no longer in business
- Bankruptcy filings
- Publicly available legal documents showing the company is no longer active

Proof of relationship status

This part only applies to you if you are married, divorced, widowed, or common law.

- Married: Marriage certificate, even if your spouse will not be immigrating with you
- Divorced: Divorce certificate if you or your spouse has ever been married in the past
- Widowed: Death certificate for your spouse

Canada will allow you to immigrate with your partner even if you're not married, but you will need to prove the validity of that common law relationship by providing:

- A completed Statutory Declaration of Common Law Union form
- Evidence of cohabitation for at least 12 continuous months including utility bills in both of your names
- Statements from joint bank accounts or credit cards
- Lease or mortgage in both of your names

If you do not include your partner, you may be permanently banned from sponsoring them in the future. If your partner is not accompanying you, you should include them on your application and indicate their status as non-accompanying.

Proof of parental status

If you're a parent of a dependent child, you will need to provide information about each of your dependent children, even if they will not be immigrating with you.

- Birth certificates for any dependent children
- Adoption certificates for any adopted dependents

If you do not include a child on your application, you may be permanently banned from sponsoring them for permanent resident status in the future.

Fees

You'll have to pay your Right of Permanent Residence fees, Express Entry fee, and biometrics fee online before your application is considered complete.

If anything in your profile has changed since you originally created your expression of interest, be sure to update it before submitting your application.

Lying or misrepresenting information on your application is a bad idea. It's easy to fudge information on a form, but lying about something that impacts your residence in a country is messing with international laws. Canada doesn't have draconian prisons, but it's still not worth the risk.

Biometrics

Most applicants are now required to submit biometrics (a photo and fingerprints) if you're between 14 and 79 years old, even if you gave your biometrics in the past and they're still valid. The IRCC has a tool to help you determine if you need to provide biometrics.

Once you've submitted your application, you'll get a letter in your myCIC account requesting your biometrics. You have 30 days to do this. You need to bring this letter and your passport to your biometrics appointment. Anyone included in your application (ie. all living immediate family members, regardless of whether they're moving to Canada or not) must also provide biometrics.

This must be done at a Visa Application Centre (VAC) or Application Support Centre (ASC). There are no VACs or ASCs in Canada, so if you are applying from within Canada you'll need to leave the country to do this. This was not required prior to 2018.

Your application will not be processed until your biometrics are submitted.

The biometrics fee is $85, with a maximum of $170 per family.

Application processing

You'll get messages in your MyCIC mailbox with occasional updates or requests for any additional information. They may even request an interview.

The IRCC aims to process applications within six months and they hit that target for most applicants. In fact, some people have their paperwork processed in only six weeks!

Applications that take longer than six months likely were missing documents (like the police check), required additional background screening, had unclear family situations (pending divorces, adoptions, or child custody issues), or required an in-person interview.

Ready for visa

About five months after I submitted my application and all of the fees, I got an email letting me know that I was "Ready for Visa." This let me know that my application was almost complete. Though this wasn't an official "approval" quite yet, I took as it as a sign that I was nearly done with the process. I was asked to mail out:

- 2 photographs for my Permanent Resident (PR) cards
- Copies of my passport
- One self-addressed stamped envelope

About a month after I this, I received my permanent resident visa, the official travel papers that granted me the right to immigrate to Canada. All told, it was almost exactly six months between when I submitted my application to when I received the paperwork I needed to actually immigrate.

How much EE cost

In addition to having money in your bank account to provide proof of funds, you'll also end up paying for just about every piece of documentation you'll need to gather as part of your application.

While your experience might be a bit different, here's an overview of what I ended up paying to prepare my application while living in the US in 2015:

Document	Single	Couple
Police Certificate	$18	$36
– Fingerprinting	$25	$50
Language Test (IELTS)	$225	$550
Education Credential Assessment	$205	$410
– Transcripts (2)	$50	$100
– Diplomas (1)	$50	$50
Medical Exam	$350	$700
– Passport Photos	$20	$40
Express Entry Fee	$395	$790
Right of Permanent Resident Fee	$350	$700
Photographs for PR card	$20	$40
Biometrics	C$85	C$170
Total	$1,708	$3,466

In 2015 biometrics were not yet required, so they are not factored into the total, but I've included it here for your reference.

There are other costs you might have to pay, depending on your situation:

- Document translation (required for any document that is not in English or French)
- Immigration representative fees
- Copies of marriage, divorce, or death certificates
- Proof of common law partnership
- Copies of birth or adoption certificates
- Additional language test to establish French fluency

Timeline

Everyone's experience will be different, but here's how the timing worked out for me:

Event	Date
Submitted Express Entry profile	18-Mar-15
IRCC confirmed that profile was received	19-Mar-15
Registered with job bank	19-Mar-15
Accepted into Express Entry	19-Mar-15
Invited to apply for Permanent Residency	27-Mar-15
Appointment with panel physician	2-Apr-15
Submitted application for Permanent Residency	13-Apr-15
IRCC confirmed that application was received	13-Apr-15
IRCC requested additional information	29-May-15
Provided additional information	29-May-15
IRCC confirmed that information was received	30-May-15
Received "Ready for Visa" email	15-Sep-15
Mailed out pictures and copies of passports	29-Sep-15
Received travel documents (invitation to immigrate)	26-Oct-15
Primary applicant declared residency	10-Dec-15
Actually moved to Toronto	15-Jan-16
Expiration date for invitation to immigrate	2-Apr-16

Document checklist and timeline

There are two different rounds of the application process. First you'll need to create your Express Entry profile on the IRCC website. Then, you'll be invited to apply for permanent residency status through one of the three economic immigration programs available through Express Entry.

I had all of the paperwork ready to go before I even created my profile since once you get started it all goes so fast. The exceptions to this are the medical exam, which you won't even be eligible to schedule until you've already been invited to apply, and biometrics, which need to be done after you submit your complete application.

What you'll need to create your profile

These are the approximate times I waited for each document required to create my profile. Keep in mind that your own wait times and costs may be a bit different. Though some things are marked as optional, they are required if you'd like to receive points for it.

	Wait Time	Cost	FSWP	CEC	FSTP
Education Credential Assessment	1-3 months	$200	✓	Optional	Optional
– diplomas	2-4 weeks	$50	✓	If needed	If needed
– school transcripts	2-4 weeks	$50	✓	Optional	Optional
Language test results	1-3 months	$225	✓	✓	✓
Passport if you don't have one	6 weeks	$50	✓	✓	✓
Travel history			✓	✓	✓
Residential history			✓	✓	✓
Job history			✓	✓	✓

What you'll need for your application

After you've been invited to apply for Express Entry, you'll need all of these documents on hand in order to submit your application.

The table below shows the approximate times that I waited to receive the documents request at this stage, as well as the approximate costs. You may find that you wait more or less time depending on where you live, went to school, and worked. The different streams have slightly different requirements.

	Wait time	Cost	FSWP	CEC	FSTC
Police certificate	3-4 months	$20	✓	✓	✓
– fingerprints	1 day	$25	✓	✓	✓
Medical exam	1-2 months	$350	✓	✓	✓
Letters from all employers for the past 10 years	1-6 months		✓		✓
Letters from all Canadian employers	1 month			✓	
Proof of funds, valid job offer, or work permit	1 weeks		✓		✓
Provincial nomination	1+ months		Optional	Optional	Optional
Proof of relationship status	1 month	$20	if needed	if needed	if needed
Proof of parental status	1 month	$20	if needed	if needed	if needed
Written job offer	1 month		Optional	Optional	Optional
Work permits, T4s, NOAs	1 day			✓	

Part Six: Landing in Canada

You've made it through the paperwork and you've officially been invited to move to the Great White North. Now what?

I always want to know what to expect, but there was very little information about the process of actually arriving at the border and becoming a legal resident of Canada. I was hoping that meant it was so easy to move that no one had bothered to write about it. The IRCC instructions make sense to me now, but before I actually did it they seemed very confusing.

The good news is that it is pretty simple, especially if you're just arriving with a few suitcases. It gets a little more complicated once you add a family and a house worth of stuff, but that's true of any move. The only things you really have to worry about are exotic pets, vehicles, and individual items over C$10k in value. Even then, you'll just want to do the research ahead of time to make sure you don't have any surprises at the border.

Your landing paperwork

Landing in Canada for the first time as a new resident doesn't necessarily mean that you have to "land" at an airport. You can just as easily drive yourself across the border, arrive on a boat, or change your status from inside the country.

If you're living outside of Canada when you receive your visa, you can enter Canada by going to any Canadian Port of Entry (POE). These are generally land crossings with the US or international airports.

If you're living in Canada already, you can update your status by making an appointment at an IRCC office. It may be simpler and faster to go to a port of entry, assuming you can legally enter the US or feel like taking an international vacation. However, recently the IRCC has put restrictions on flagpoling at major POEs, like at Niagara Falls, through a pilot program to reduce wait times at the border. Check CBSA restrictions at your intended POE before you go, since the CBSA tends to institute these policies without making a public announcement first.

In addition to the visa and my passport, I brought all of the documents that were submitted with my application. You probably won't need to show any of this stuff, but you could be required to. Technically, they can ask for original documents for anything you submitted with your application and turn you away if you don't present them. This is rare, but I've met people who've had this happen. If it happens to you, you can try again before your visa expires. That's a lot easier to do if you're entering by land.

There are things you absolutely need to have with you at the border, like your visa and your passport.

If you're bringing your stuff with you to Canada, you need:
- BSF186 form for goods on your person (two copies)
- BSF186 form for goods to follow (two copies)

I'll go over the BSF186 forms and how to actually move your things later on.

These papers probably won't be required, but you'll want to have with you if they were in your application:
- Sealed letter from your medical exam
- Police certificate
- Birth certificate
- Language test results
- Education credential assessment
- Diplomas
- Proof of funds
- Verification of your work history
- Proof of relationship status, if applicable
- Proof of parental status, if applicable
- Written job offer, if you have one

Landing paperwork for EE

When you get a letter in the mail saying your application for permanent residence in Canada has been approved, you'll also get a Confirmation of Permanent Residence (CoPR) paper for yourself and any other family members that you applied to immigrate with. The CoPR paper is very important, though it's not obvious by looking at it. This is your permanent resident visa.

You aren't a permanent resident yet, even with your PR visa. The final step is signing the paper in front of a border agent during your final immigration interview.

The CoPR is a single legal-sized piece of paper with your personal details and a big stamp across it that says "NOT VALID FOR TRAVEL." It actually looks a bit like a temporary driver's license. Keep this in a safe place – Canadian customs officers will not allow you to cross the border and declare that you are moving to Canada without your CoPR.

Take careful note of the "valid to" date, which will be exactly one year from when your panel physician submitted the results of your medical exam. You absolutely must declare landing in Canada before this date passes. The IRCC is clear that this cannot be extended for any reason.

You can declare landing even if you plan to return to your home country to finalize your move. The border agents I spoke to said that's pretty common. You may want to return to sell your home, finish up the school year, or do other things to wrap up life in your old country. You can't, however, declare landing and then not actually move. Or you can, but you'll lose your PR status.

If you applied to immigrate with other members of your family, you can land before they do, but they can't land before the primary applicant. They can, however, enter Canada as a visitor and return to declare landing after you've become a permanent resident.

Every family member who is coming with you to Canada needs to declare landing before their CoPR expires.

If your family situation has changed since you applied, you will have to make that declaration before you immigrate. If you've gotten married, divorced, entered into a common law relationship, had a new baby, or adopted a child since you submitted your application, let the IRCC know as soon as possible so that they can adjust your invitation accordingly. This will probably delay your ability to move.

Your official Permanent Resident card will arrive in the mail at the address you list on the CoPR form in about 6-8 weeks. Until then, the CoPR form will serve as both your temporary proof of permanent resident status and a record of your landing in Canada.

The CoPR is very important! If you decide later on to apply for Canadian citizenship you will need to submit the CoPR document as proof of when you landed in Canada, so keep it in a safe place.

Flying into Canada

I decided to declare landing at Toronto Pearson Airport and paid a moving company to bring all of my stuff up later. Driving a moving truck from Brooklyn to Toronto with two cats was not something I wanted to deal with.

At the airport, the first customs agent asked me what my current status was in Canada and I explained that I was declaring myself a landed immigrant. I needed to show my completed customs declaration card, passport, and visa document at this initial stage.

If you've ever flown into Canada you'll have filled out a customs declaration card on the airplane on which you'll identify yourself as a visitor or resident. There's no "settler" option. The customs agent I spoke to explained that since I wasn't yet living in Canada, I should put my most recent US address and mark myself as a Canadian resident.

Then, I was directed to a second customs clearing area.

Customs

The secondary customs area is where I spoke with a border patrol agent about my plans to move to Canada. They reviewed my visa and passport, verified me in their system, and asked me general questions about my life. This is also where they will review your biometrics to ensure they match the biometrics on your application.

I was asked why I decided to move to Canada, where I was going to be living, and what I did for work. Other people report being asked if they've ever been convicted of a crime, how long it took them to do the application, if they'd ever been deported, and even if they'd called their parents to let them know they'd landed safely.

The customs agent filled out my visa form, the CoPR, with my landing information.

Depending on what time you arrive at the airport, the secondary customs area might be empty or crowded. You might think it's best to avoid peak times, but if you arrive at an off time, you might miss out on some of the settlement services at the airport and have border agents who aren't as experienced.

I arrived at a peak time, so I waited in line for a while to talk to a customs agent. However, because I was able to get my SIN and a bunch of settlement information (and a bag of welcome goodies!) it saved me time in the long run.

If you want to ask a human being some quick questions about enrolling your kids in school, setting up a bank account, or other settlement questions, you'll have an opportunity to do so at the airport. If they don't have the answer, you'll be directed to the right agency to find assistance.

Social Insurance Number

The customs agent might not tell you this, but you can probably get your new Social Insurance Number (SIN) at the airport. This is the number you will need to access government benefits and programs like health insurance. You'll also need it to fill out your taxes.

At Toronto Pearson they do this right in the customs area within a few minutes and you'll have the opportunity to ask questions of staff who are experts in immigration and settling.

Declaring goods

After I finished up at the secondary customs clearing area and got my SIN, I was let out at the luggage area of the airport.

The final step of landing is declaring goods. You know how you're always asked if you have goods to declare? Today you have things to declare, even if you're not bringing them with you right now. Especially if you're not bringing them with you right now.

When you go to exit and hand your customs declaration card to the agent, let that person know that you need to declare goods. If you don't have them with you right now, tell them you are a new resident and have goods to follow. They should then direct you to a final clearance area where you will declare your goods and get your BSF186 document or list of items stamped. Hold on to this. If you're importing goods at a later date, you will need to show this document when you bring your goods across the border to avoid paying duties.

If you don't get your BSF186 or goods list stamped at the airport, you will not be able to take advantage of duty exemptions for new residents. If you're thinking you might bring things over at any point in the future, it's worth creating a goods to follow list, which does not expire. It doesn't require you to actually import the items, but it allows you to bring them over duty free in the future.

Driving into Canada

Some land border crossings are putting restrictions on when foreign nationals can process their work permits, process study permits, and validate their permanent resident status. Check with CSBA if there are restrictions at the port of entry you plan on using so you don't find this out the hard way.

People who are already in Canada typically 'flagpole' to adjust their status if they're already in Canada. This is when you enter the US at a land crossing and then immediately re-enter Canada. This allows you to simply show up at a port of entry to get your status changed by a border agent. If you aren't allowed to flagpole, border agents will allow you to re-enter Canada under your current status (assuming that's an option) and apply for an appointment to have your status adjusted inside the country.

The other option for people changing their status from within Canada is to make an appointment with the nearest immigration office so you can have your 'landing' interview inside of Canada.

At the port of entry, tell the customs agent that you're landing in Canada as a new resident. You'll be asked to drive your vehicle to a second checkpoint where you will be interviewed by a customs agent who will go over all of your documents.

If you're taking a bus across the border, you'll want to make sure you can take a later bus the rest of the way, since your original bus will not wait for you.

You'll need your BSF186 or goods list ready for any of your things you're bringing into the country with you. If you're not bringing your things across the border right now, you'll need to have a BSF186 form for goods to follow. They'll stamp it and you'll need this when you do bring your things into the country.

If you now have the right to work in Canada, you'll need to visit your local Service Canada location to get your Social Insurance Number (SIN). Be sure to take your passport and visa document with you when you go.

Importing your worldly possessions

If you're moving to Canada you'll need a list of all of the items you're importing for your personal use. You'll need this on your BSF186 form, previously known as a B4. While the name CBSA uses has changed, it's essentially the same form and has both identification numbers on it.

This requirement is enforced unevenly by customs agents. Some people are never asked to show their lists. Others who show up without lists are forced to unpack at the border and create a list right then and there. I'd much rather have a list and not need it.

Moving as a temporary resident

If you have a vacation home in Canada, you have one shot to bring in household and personal items. You can't sell any of these items for at least a year. You'll need to show that you've purchased a property recently or have a least for three years or longer. You'll complete the BSF186 as a "seasonal resident."

Technically, you're not supposed to sell or get rid of anything you import without customs approval. However, this is really only an issue for high-value items. Declutter last season's clothes? Go ahead. Sell your incredibly rare vintage guitar? Check first. You may be required to pay duty.

Not everything is duty free. Any single item that's over C$10k in value will be taxed on the excess (ie. the value over $10k). Some items require special permission to bring into Canada, like plants. Check the CBSA website for complete details.

Immigrating

If you're immigrating, you'll need to complete the BSF186, as a "settler." You don't need to have everything you own with you the day you arrive in Canada as a new resident.

After you declare landing, you are free to return to your home country whenever you want and can cross back into Canada, bringing more stuff with you each time. If you do this, you will need to make sure that you have your stamped BSF186 form with you every single time you cross the border with additional belongings. Once you bring something into Canada, you can bring it back and forth across the border without needing to declare it again.

If you are bringing anything that was not included on the BSF186 form, you will need to declare it at the border and pay any associated taxes you may owe. You're better off packing any items not on the BSF186 in one section you can access easily if you need to show them to a customs officer. Of course, if the value of what you're bringing in is under your personal exception, you won't have to declare them. Currently, the personal exemption is C$800 if you've been out of Canada for 48 hours or more.

Remember that the BSF186 is a way to avoid paying taxes and anything that was not already declared can be taxed. The customs officials will not be happy if they realize you're trying to sneak additional items into the country without paying the appropriate taxes on them.

While in theory you can make as many trips as are needed, I don't suggest making more than one or two trips with belongings you need to declare. You will need to go through the entire customs process each time, which can take a few hours.

Check the CBSA website for complete details on what you can import duty free and what the restrictions are.

Vehicles

You can probably bring your car with you when you move. The Register of Imported Vehicles explains everything you need to know about the import process. It will need to meet Canadian safety standards if it's less than 15 years old. There is a $75 inspection fee and handling charges.

If you're on a temporary visa, you can bring an ineligible car into Canada as long as you take it with you when you leave the country. You cannot sell it or give it away in Canada.

If you have leased or financed your car, you will first need to get in touch with the company you've leased or financed it from to find out if you can bring it to Canada with you. If you can, you'll need the original Certificate of Title along with an original letter from the company that authorizes the import and identifies the car and VIN.

Pets

Bringing your pets into Canada is a pretty simple process. Canada does not require a quarantine period for domestic cats and dogs coming from most countries, but you will need to prove that they are in good health.

If you're not coming from a rabies-free country, you will need to bring a current rabies vaccination certificate. While it's not specifically required by customs, you will probably want to have any recent paperwork from your veterinarian as well, just in case.

When you cross a border with a pet, either to immigrate or just to visit, your pets will be inspected by a customs agent to make sure that the paperwork is valid and they appear to be in good health. You might be asked to pay an inspection fee for each animal. I wasn't asked to pay this.

The government reserves the right to refuse to allow an animal to enter the country if it does not meet the necessary requirements. The IRCC website has a handy overview of the different requirements for each type of animal that you might want to bring with you.

One more issue is breed specific regulations. Pit bulls are banned in Ontario and Winnipeg, Manitoba.

Flying with a small pet

If you're flying, most airlines will allow you to book a spot for your pet so long as you let them know when you are booking the tickets. There's usually a fee for this and restrictions regarding the weight and carrier.

Some airlines will require you to provide veterinarian paperwork. Make sure you ask about this when you book the flight so that you can make sure you have everything you'll need.

Getting a pet through airport security

If you fly often, you'll know that security is a little different at every airport, and often different each time you fly.

US security requires that you take your pet out of the carrier and physically walk them through the metal detector while they scan the carrier. Because I was flying with cats, I was very worried about this part. I got a harness and leash for my cats, but since cats are a liquid, I'm pretty sure they could have escaped if they wanted to. Luckily, my cats were so freaked out by the whole situation that they didn't try to move at all. Make sure your pet harness doesn't have any pieces that would set off the metal detector.

Don't surprise TSA agents. Give them a heads up as you walk up and let them know that you have an animal and ask them how they want you to proceed. The TSA agents were really friendly and helpful when I brought my cats.

Get yourself ready to walk through security (place your bags on the conveyor belt, take off your shoes and belt, take your laptop and liquids out of your bag, empty your pockets, etc.). This is an excellent day to wear slip on shoes and not have a belt. The more prepared you are for this part the better. While holding your pet, wait for TSA to give you the go ahead to walk through the metal detector.

Pets on a plane

It should go without saying that your pet needs to remain in the carrier for the duration of the trip. Remember that not everyone loves pets as much as you do and many people are allergic to pets. Some people are mortally afraid of both flying and animals, so try to be considerate.

When you get on the plane, let the flight attendants know that you have an animal so they can make things easy for you. Pet carriers must be kept under the seat. My cats were so terrified they didn't move or make a sound for the (mercifully short) flight. They were fine and happy to explore as soon as they arrived at their new home.

Getting your pet through customs

Let customs know that you have a pet. You'll be taken to a separate clearing area where a customs agent will inspect your pet to make sure everything is in order. Usually this is just a visual check to make sure the animal isn't obviously sick. You may also be asked for proof of vaccinations.

This part was very quick and easy. The agents just spent a minute talking about how cute my cats were and sent us on our way.

Wedding presents

You can bring your wedding presents into Canada duty free within three months of your wedding (either before or after you get married).

Inheritance

If you inherit goods while you're a resident of Canada, you can generally import them duty free as long as you provide a copy of the estate documents and the death certificate. The BSF186 refers to this as a "beneficiary" import.

The BSF186 form

Canada requires that you declare all of your goods on a Personal Affects Accounting Document, aka the BSF186 form. Anything not included on your BSF186 will be taxed at normal import rates.

You can create a single BSF186 for your family or each adult can have their own.

If you are moving up with all of your things, then you only need a single BSF186 for all of your accompanying goods. If you are landing with just a few pieces of luggage and plan to move all of your stuff up at a later date, then you will need two BSF186 forms:

- Goods Accompanying: This is a list of all the things you have with you on the day that you land. This could be a single bag, multiple pieces of checked luggage, or everything you own.
- Goods to Follow: This is a list of all the things you plan to bring into Canada in the future. If you're going to bring all of your stuff into Canada a few days or decades in the future you will need to let customs know the first time you land. If you don't declare them at this time you could be taxed on them later.

Looking at the form, you'll see that there are only eight lines to list goods. Use this section to list up to eight categories. For example:

Item	Description of goods (include serial numbers, if applicable)	Value (CDN Dollars)
1	Furniture	$3,000
2	Kitchen	$2,000
3	Clothing	$4,000
4	Electronics	$5,000
5	Linens	$1,000
6	Books	$2,000
7	Décor	$2,000
8		

You can create whatever categories make sense for you.

I made a list of items in each category with the approximate value. Some people advise you to list garage sale values, others recommend listing replacement costs. Technically, you don't need to provide values unless you're asked for them, but I would rather not have to guess while I'm at customs.

For each list, include the category, category number from the list you made on the BSF186 form, your full legal name, a description of the item, quantity, and approximate value in Canadian dollars.

You will also need to include the make, model, and serial number for each item, if it has one. This is usually for things like electronics and sports equipment. For items like high-value jewelry and art, they may require that you include a photo of the item. Generally, they don't really care about any item valued at less than a few thousand dollars.

Here's an example of how I made the category lists:

GOODS TO FOLLOW				
CATEGORY: Furniture				
MY NAME				
No.	Item Description	Serial #	Quantity	Value (CAD)
1	Kitchen chairs		4	$100
2	Kitchen table		1	$300
3	Armchair		2	$400
4	Bookcase		4	$550
5	Filing cabinet		1	$250

You don't need to itemize everything you own. You can group things together for the sake of simplicity. For example:

No.	Item Description	Serial #	Quantity	Value (CAD)
1	Boxes of books		6	$300
2	Boxes of toiletries		3	$150
3	Boxes of tools		3	$500

The only things that should be listed individually are high value items. Unless you have designer clothes that would fetch a tidy sum at resale, you can simply list the number of boxes.

When you're done, print out two copies of each category list along with two copies of each BSF186. The CBSA will keep one and give the other back to you.

There is no limit on the amount of time you have to import things on your goods to follow list. However, once the list is stamped by customs you cannot add anything to it.

This list will be useful when you get renters or homeowners insurance, since you now have a government approved list of everything you own and its value.

Hiring movers to move you from the US

You can't hire a random guy with a van to move your stuff across an international border. Only certain companies are properly licensed to do this. They'll as for a copy of your passport and CoPR document when you book your move.

Customs for goods to follow

When you landed as a new resident and declared that you had goods to follow, the customs agent reviewed your list of goods and entered it all into their database. They're now going to cross reference the goods that you actually import with the goods that you declared when you land. You'll need the paperwork with you.

Even if you hire a moving company, you will still need to physically sign for and receive your belongings after they are brought across the border. You can either meet the movers at the Canadian border or at a CBSA sufferance office.

Whichever way you go about this, make sure that you get very specific instructions from your moving company about where, when, and how to meet them. Also ask about the cost, both for moving and fees associated with customs.

Either way, you will be interviewed by a customs agent and be asked to show your passport, visa document, and stamped BSF186 form. The CBSA will stamp your BSF186 form and mark your goods as arrived.

They will also give you a completed and stamped A8A form, the Customs Cargo Control Document. This verifies that your goods were allowed into the country and cleared by customs.

It's possible that customs will go through everything in your truck and compare it to the list. In my case, they didn't even open the truck. It still took about two hours.

Part Seven: Moving to Québec

Québec has different immigration requirements than the rest of the provinces. Unfortunately, in practical terms, this just means that moving to Québec has extra hurdles.

Do you need to speak French?

Over 80% of people in Québec speak French, but plenty of them speak English as well. While people who speak conversational French are favored over Anglophiles, it's not required that you speak French before you move to Québec and you don't need to speak French to qualify for their immigration programs.

You're encouraged to spend time learning French online or take classes before you leave your home country in order to help you integrate more quickly. If you take language classes in your current country of residence prior to immigrating, you may be able to have some or all of the fee reimbursed. Once you're in Québec, you'll have access to French courses free of charge and possibly even financial aid to help you take time off to attend classes.

Why is there so much conflicting information out there?

From 2015 to 2017, immigration programs in Canada underwent a tremendous number of changes as the federal government switched from paper applications to an online system in several phases and then tweaked them to make them easier to use. This is why my ex-wife and I wrote the first edition of this book, because all the information we found on the immigration process was about a system that no longer existed.

Quebec is going through that process currently, having just moved their largest immigration program to an online system. Right now the federal portion of that program is still done on paper, as are Quebec's other immigration programs.

Because things are changing rapidly, you should be extra careful to verify that the information you're reading here is still accurate, even if it's less than a year old.

Living and working in Québec temporarily

There are two primary ways you can live in Québec on a temporary basis: going to school or getting a work permit.

Going (back) to school

Once you choose a school, apply, and are accepted, the school will guide you through the process of getting a student visa. You'll need to provide proof that you can support yourself while you go to school.

As a student in Québec, you're agreeing that:

- Studying will be your principal activity for the entire time you're in Québec,
- You will supply your own health insurance coverage, and
- You will cover your own tuition, transportation costs (to and from Canada), living expenses, and any other costs.

You don't need to get a student visa for programs lasting six months or less.

Many students choose to extend their stay after graduation or immigrate permanently. You can do this by getting a post-graduation work permit and eventually applying for permanent resident status.

Find a job

Once you have a job offer in Québec, you and your employer have to take steps to make it legal. Your employer will work with Ministère de l'Immigration, de la Diversité et de l'Inclusion to complete the paperwork required, which will include demonstrating that they were unable to find a local employee to do the job. Your work permit will be specific to that employer.

Any time you extend your employment contract or change jobs, you'll need to file a new work authorization application.

Becoming a permanent resident in Québec

If you qualify for family sponsorship and you wish to live in Québec, you apply through the IRCC like any other applicant and will be directed to complete an additional application through the Ministère de l'Immigration, de la Diversité et de l'Inclusion (MIDI).

Québec has its own visa and immigration procedures for economic immigration programs. Thus, for these programs you apply through MIDI first and then apply for federal approval through the IRCC.

Once you are living in Canada as a permanent resident, there are no restrictions on where you can live. However, it's frowned upon to apply to live in one province and immediately move to another. If you apply for PR through a Provincial Nomination Program, you could face consequences if you move to another province right away.

Is moving to Québec right for you?

The Ministère de l'Immigration, de la Diversité et de l'Inclusion offers free online and in-person information sessions to explain what it's like to live, work, and go to school in Québec and goes over the immigration process. These are offered in several languages and can be scheduled online.

Common values

Once you receive your Certificat de sélection du Québec (CSQ) you'll need to sign the Declaration on the Common Values of Québec Society. These values are:

- Speaking French is a necessity
- A free and democratic society
- A society enriched by its diversity
- A society based on the rule of law
- Political and religious powers are separate
- Men and women have the same rights
- The exercise of human rights and freedoms must respect the rights and freedoms of others and the general well-being

Being sponsored by a resident of Québec

If your sponsor lives in Québec or you plan to live in Québec once you're granted residency, you'll need to complete an extra step after the IRCC approves your federal application. You'll need to obtain a Québec Selection

Certificate (CSQ) from the Ministère de l'Immigration, de la Diversité et de l'Inclusion (MIDI). As of July 2019, this is all done on paper.

MIDI encourages you to prepare your CSQ application as you gather documents for your IRCC application and while you wait to hear from the IRCC. This way you can submit your CSQ application as soon as you are able to and can avoid unnecessary delays.

What you have to do

You need to fill out the Demande de sélection permanente – Catégorie du regroupement familial (Application for permanent selection – Family reunification class). This application is available only in French.

When your application is complete you need to give it to your sponsor, who will submit it to MIDI on your behalf.

What your sponsor has to do

Your sponsor has to complete an Undertaking Kit, legally agreeing to be financially responsible for you. Their legal responsibilities and the forms required differ based on their relationship to you. They also need to demonstrate that they are capable of providing for you financially and, of course, they need to pay an application fee.

The undertaking kit, your application, all required documents, and payment information are all submitted to MIDI together.

MIDI provides a guide for sponsors, which is only in French.

When you have your CSQ

MIDI's will directly contact the Canadian visa office for your country with their decision regarding your CSQ application. If your CSQ is issued, you will be issued a CoPR and a visa (if your nationality requires a visa to enter Canada). Congratulations, you can finally go to a port of entry to declare yourself a landed immigrant!

The Québec Skilled Worker Program

The Québec Skilled Worker Program (QSWP) has undergone many well publicized changes recently (like when they trashed the backlog of 18k applications and started fresh) and it now bears a striking resemblance to Express Entry. However, it's an entirely separate system.

Instead of applying through myCIC, you use the Arrima system. The Arrima system is only available in French. Instructions and requirements are kept up to date in French. When accessing English pages on the MIDI website you will likely find that they have a notice telling you to view the

French version for accurate information, because the English instructions are out of date.

This system launched in September 2018, so any instructions from before that time are no longer accurate.

How does the QSWP work?

1. You create a free profile (your "expression of interest") and are entered into a pool of candidates.
2. Candidates with the highest scores are selected from the pool and invited to apply. You then have 60 days to gather documents and submit your application for a Certificat de sélection du Québec (CSQ).
3. When you have been granted a CSQ, you submit a paper application for permanent residence to the federal government. You likely also need to submit biometrics and may have an interview.
4. When your federal application has been approved, you receive a Confirmation of Permanent Residence (CoPR) form and a visa (if your country of nationality requires a visa). You present this to a government official at a port of entry and become a permanent resident.

QSWP basic requirements

In order to qualify to submit an expression of interest for the QSWP, you need to be over the age of 18, have a secondary school (high school) general diploma, and show proof of settlement funds.

For a single person in 2019, the required proof of funds is just over C$3k. That may be the minimum amount required by the program, but it would be a struggle to relocate to a new country with so little money, especially without a job offer lined up and family to stay with.

While Québec manages its own immigration programs, you must still meet all of the federal requirements. Thus, if you're inadmissible to Canada, your application will be rejected.

Like Express Entry, you do not need a qualifying job offer to get PR through the QSWP. However, having a qualifying job offer increases your chances of being issued an Invitation to Apply (ITA) and having a successful application.

Speaking French is not a requirement, but is highly encouraged. The application and most instructions are only available in French.

Who gets priority?

There are three types of people whose Arrima profiles get priority processing in the new QSWP system:

- people with a qualifying job offer from an employer in Québec
- people whose CSQ application was thrown out when they switched to the new system and who were temporary residents of Quebec when they applied
- people whose CSQ application was thrown out when they switched to the new system and who were in Québec on a student visa or a temporary work permit when they applied

When Arrima was first launched in 2018, only 5k profiles were accepted. These three groups were not subject to the caps. Participants in the Québec Experience Program (Programme de l'expérience québécoise or PEQ) were also exempt from the cap.

Who can come with me?

Your spouse (or common-law partner) and dependent children should be included in your expression of interest and final application. Everyone who is included on your application will receive permanent resident status once you become landed immigrants.

If you are planning on immigrating without your spouse or common-law partner, you do not need to include them in your expression of interest profile. If you get an ITA, you would need to include them as a non-accompanying spouse on your application. If you would like them to join you later, you will need to go through the sponsorship process.

If you wish to immigrate with your child (or children) but without the other parent, you will need to demonstrate that you have legal permission from the other parent.

Do I need an immigration attorney?

Many people hire immigration representatives to help them. Going through the process on your own involves a lot of paperwork, a lot of annoying online forms, and a lot of checking to make sure you filled things out correctly. It's very tedious and navigating this process in French (or using a translation tool) can be challenging.

You know how much your time is worth and how comfortable you are outsourcing important tasks. Like Express Entry, Arrima is designed to be used without an immigration consultant or attorney.

Selection criteria

You're awarded points based on your:

- age
- language proficiency
- time spent in Québec and/or family in Québec
- financial self-sufficiency
- education
- area of training
- work experience
- qualifying job offer
- the characteristics of your spouse or common-law partner
- your accompanying children (as in, if you have them and how many)

There is a potential total of 120 points. A single person needs at least 50 points. The minimum for candidates with a spouse or common-law partner is 59 points.

If you're between 18 and 35 years old, you get the maximum number of points for age. The number of points awarded begins dropping at 36 until you receive zero points for being 43 or older. This is a program designed to bring young skilled workers into the country, so the older you are, the more impressive your other factors need to be. Once you receive an ITA, your ages (and the ages of accompanying family members) are 'locked in' and the number of points awarded for your age does not change.

Your French gets you points from the High Intermediate (B2) level and above. You are awarded a smaller number of points for speaking English at the Intermediate (CLB 5-8) or above. You will only be awarded points based on a recognized language exam, even if English or French is your native language or you have completed a diploma in the language.

You get a point for having spent more than two weeks in Québec. Having stayed for three months or more, gone to school, or worked in Québec will get you even more points.

You will get points if you have a spouse or common-law partner in Québec. You will also get points for having a child, parent, sibling, or grandparent in Québec.

Your financial self-sufficiency is a single point and it's the yes/no question of having the required proof of settlement funds.

You're required to have a secondary school diploma and will receive an increasing number of points for higher levels of education. Your area of specialization is not taken into account here, it is evaluated in the area of training section.

The government of Québec periodically releases a list of areas of training that outlines the number of points awarded for different types of degrees, certifications, and other diplomas. The official list is only available in French, although several websites provide translated versions.

If the list of areas of training is updated after you submit your EOA to the pool or after you submit your application, the number of points you are awarded may change.

You are awarded points for your paid work experience, with points allocated for amounts of time ranging from six months to 48 months or more. This is full-time work or the part-time equivalent.

If you have a qualifying job offer you will receive points for that. The number of points awarded depends on the geographic region the position is located in, with Montreal resulting in the fewest points.

If you have a spouse or common-law partner, you will get points based on their age, language, education, and area of training.

You get points for having dependent children, with more points awarded for children under 13.

You can calculate your score based on information from the Ministère de l'Immigration, de la Diversité et de l'Inclusion website or use a third-party score calculator.

Document checklist

Québec

You will be provided with a personalized document checklist by MIDI when you receive your ITA. However, some documents may take more than 60 days to procure, so it is helpful to be prepared. You are likely to need:
- Birth certificates for all applicants
- Passports for all applicants
- Marriage certificate or proof of common-law partnership
- Certified true copies of diplomas and transcripts
- Verification of work history (similar to that required for EE)
- Language exam(s)

Many of the documents required in order to apply for the QSWP must be certified true copies. Documents that are not in English or French must be translated by a recognized translator. Original documents and translated copies must both be provided. The document must be translated in its entirety.

Federal

- Biometrics
- Police certificate(s)
- Medical exam

Language tests

You have to take a language exam to demonstrate your proficiency in French and/or English if you want to get points for it.

For French, you can use scores for any of these exams:

- Test d'Evaluation du Français (TEF/TEF Canada)
- Test d'Evaluation du français adapté pour le Québec (TEFaQ)
- Test de connaissance du français (TCF)
- Test de connaissance du français pour le Québec (TCFQ)
- Diplôme d'études en langue française (DELF/DALF)

For English, they use the International English Language Testing System (IELTS).

All of these exam scores expire after two years. Your score needs to be valid when it's submitted, but it is still accepted if it expires while your application is being processed.

Step-by-step instructions

Submit an expression of interest

No documentation is required at this time. However, if you are selected from the applicant pool you will need to provide documentation to verify all information in your profile within 60 days.

You can update information in your EOI profile in Arrima at any time, even if you've already submitted it. Changes must be submitted within 30 days of the event (as in, if you earn a degree you need to update your profile within 30 days of it being awarded).

Your Arrima profile expires after 365 days. If you are not selected and issued an ITA in that time, you can create a new profile.

Because the QSWP and EE are separate systems, you can create profiles for both to increase your odds of being selected.

Receive your invitation to apply

If you are selected from the pool, you'll be invited to apply (ITA) for a Québec Selection Certificate (Certificat de sélection du Québec, or CSQ). You have 60 days to submit your application. You will be provided with a personalized documentation checklist.

It is advisable to begin gathering documents before getting an ITA or you could easily run out of time and have to begin the process over again. While you won't have your personalized documentation checklist until you get your ITA, it's not terribly difficult to guess at what documents they will require.

If your ITA expires before you submit your complete application, you can simply submit a new expression of interest.

Request your CSQ

Once you've been invited to apply, you submit your application for a CSQ using the Mon projet Québec platform. This is where you upload documents to verify the information you provided in your expression of interest.

The final step in submitting your application for a CSQ is to pay the fees.

Now you wait. You can track your application and keep it up to date on Mon projet Québec.

Once you have your CSQ you can move on to the next step.

Submit your application for federal immigration

Now that you've been approved by Québec and have your CSQ, you need federal approval.

Québec has already assessed your likelihood to be economically and socially successful as an immigrant. The federal government is primarily concerned with confirming that you are admissible to Canada. They evaluate your medical exam and perform a security check.

The medical exam requirements are the same as for the EE system.

Your application needs to be mailed to the Case Processing Centre in Sydney, Nova Scotia:

Centralized Intake Office – Québec Skilled Workers (QSW)
P.O. BOX 8888
Sydney, NS B1P 0C9
Canada

You need to pay your application fees and biometrics fees when you submit the application or it will not be processed. This must be done online. You do not have to pay your right of permanent residence fees until your application is approved.

If your application is found to be incomplete it will be returned to you. You can add in any missing information and resubmit it without having to pay additional fees.

You will probably be required to submit biometrics: a photo and fingerprints. This must be done at a Visa Application Centre (VAC) or Application Support Centre (ASC). This was not required prior to 2018.

The IRCC has a tool to help you determine if you need to provide biometrics.

During this time the IRCC may request additional documents or require you to have an interview.

Wait for the final approval

You can begin to prepare for your move while you wait for the IRCC to process your application.

Québec offers several tools, in French only, for holders of a CSQ. The Service d'intégration en ligne has forums, chat rooms, and loads of information about the integration into Québec life. There are also online French courses, information on getting your qualifications recognized, and a job placement tool.

You can check your application status online while it's being processed. The IRCC may contact you for more information.

It's important to keep your information current with the IRCC. Contact the IRCC and update your information if:

- Your address, telephone number, email address, or any other contact information you've provided has changed
- You get married or divorced, or if you begin or end a common-law partnership
- You have a child, adopt a child, or a child dies

Any situation where you are ending a partnership or child custody is unclear will delay your application.

Receive your confirmation of PR and visa

When you get a letter in the mail saying your application for permanent residence in Canada has been approved, you'll also get a Confirmation of Permanent Residence (CoPR) paper for yourself and any other family members that you applied to immigrate with. The CoPR paper is very important, though it's not obvious by looking at it. This is your permanent resident visa.

If you're coming from a country that requires a visa to enter Canada, you'll also receive a visa for that.

You aren't a permanent resident yet, even with your CoPR. The final step is when you sign the paper in front of a border agent during your final immigration interview.

The CoPR is a single legal-sized piece of paper with your personal details and a big stamp across it that says "NOT VALID FOR TRAVEL." It actually looks a bit like a temporary driver's license. Keep this in a safe place –

Canadian customs officers will not allow you to cross the border and declare that you are moving to Canada without your CoPR.

Take careful note of the "valid to" date, which will be exactly one year from when your panel physician submitted the results of your medical exam. You absolutely must declare landing in Canada before this date passes. The IRCC is clear that this cannot be extended for any reason.

If you applied to immigrate with other members of your family, you can land before they do, but they can't land before the primary applicant. They can, however, enter Canada as a visitor and return to declare landing after you've become a permanent resident.

Every family member who is coming with you to Canada needs to declare landing before their CoPR expires.

If your spouse or children do not declare landing before their CoPR expires, you will have to go through the family sponsorship process for them to join you in Canada.

Timeline & fees

The goal is for applications to be processed within 12 months. In July 2019 the anticipated processing time was 15 to 17 months.

You can check application processing times for the federal portion of the application on the IRCC website.

- Québec application processing fee: $798 for the principal applicant / $171 for each accompanying family member
- Federal application processing fee: $550 per adult
- Right of permanent residence fee: $490 per adult
- Federal fees for dependent child: $150 per child
- Biometrics: $85 per person / $170 maximum per family

Programme de l'expérience Québécoise

Once you've studied or worked in Québec, you can participate in Québec Experience Program (Programme de l'expérience Québécoise or PEQ). Maybe. This program is on hold as of July 2019, possibly because if you qualify for PEQ, you also qualify for the Québec Skilled Worker Program (QSWP).

Let's hope that they bring it back, because:
- you could prove language proficiency without having to take an exam, and
- processing time for PEQ applications was 20 days or less.

Moving to Québec through Express Entry

People sometimes refer to the QSWP as "Quebec Express Entry," but the QSWP and EE are entirely separate systems managed by different organizations.

If you take the IRCC test to find out if you're eligible to apply for Express Entry and indicate that you intend to move to Québec, you'll get a message letting you know that you don't qualify for Express Entry. If you intend to move to Québec, you'll need to submit your intent directly to Québec through the QSWP.

Other options

Aside from the QSWP, Québec offers three ways for people to become permanent residents of Québec.

The documents required and their formats differ for each program. Any documents not in French or English have to be translated by an approved translator.

It's relatively likely that you'll be asked to have an interview with immigration officers. These take place around Canada at various times of the year and last about an hour and a half.

The Québec Immigrant Investor Program, Entrepreneur Program, and Self-Employed Workers Program all provide pathways to citizenship. These programs only accept a limited number of applicants, but people with advanced intermediate French proficiency are exempt from the cap and receive priority processing.

Québec Immigrant Investor Program

To participate in this program you (and your partner, if applicable), must:
- Have at least C$2 million of legally acquired net assets
- Have at least two years of professional management experience
- Make a five year investment of C$1.2 million with Investissement Québec - Immigrants Investisseurs Inc. and sign an investment agreement with a financial intermediary authorized to participate in the Investor Program
- Intend to settle in Québec

Québec Entrepreneur Program

If you plan on starting, relocating, or purchasing a business in Québec, you may qualify for the Québec Entrepreneur Program.
- Stream 1 requires support from a business incubator, business accelerator, or university entrepreneurship center.
- Stream 2 requires:

- a deposit of C$300k for businesses in Montreal or C$200k outside of Montreal
- a legally acquired net worth of at least C$900k

There are additional requirements, including regarding what type of businesses qualify and the percentage of ownership. You'll need to present a business plan to MIDI.

Québec Self Employed Workers Program

If you plan on creating your own job, you may qualify for the Self-Employed Workers Program. You'll need:
- to have at least two years of professional experience as a self-employed worker in the trade you wish to practice
- legally acquired net assets of at least C$100k
- to make a deposit of C25k or C$50k

When evaluating your application, MIDI will take your ties to Québec, financial self-sufficiency, language skills, work experience, and the factors of your partner into consideration.

Landing in Montreal

When you're within 30 days of your arrival in Canada, you can set up an appointment to get help with settling in Québec.

At the airport, the first customs agent you talk to will ask you what your current status is in Canada. This is when you explain that you are declaring landing as a new permanent resident. You will need to show your completed customs declaration card, passport, and visa document at this initial stage.

They will direct you to a secondary screening area where you will show your CoPR, your biometrics will be verified, and your luggage may be searched. See the information in the main Landing in Canada section for information on bringing your belongings into Canada.

A second customs agent will sign your CoPR form and return it to you. You are now a permanent resident of Canada. Congratulations!

Most immigrants declaring landing in Québec fly into Montreal. Immigration-Québec's reception service located on the first floor of the restricted area for international arrivals, in the room called Immigration 2 – Accueil Québec. The Immigration-Québec reception service is generally open from noon to midnight. They will provide you with information on getting settled in Québec.

If you arrive outside of their opening hours, arrive at a different port of entry, or have additional questions, you can contact them at 514-864-9191 or 1-877-864-9191 (toll-free).

Getting your PR card

Your official Permanent Resident card will arrive in the mail at the address you list on the CoPR form in about 6-8 weeks. Until then, the CoPR form will serve as both your temporary proof of permanent resident status and a record of your landing in Canada.

Part Eight: Your first weeks in Canada

You've finally an official resident of Canada! There's a few things you'll need to take care of within the first few weeks, like applying for a SIN, signing up for provincial health insurance, and getting a driver's license.

Canadian provinces and territories each have slightly different processes for these things, but the general idea is the same. I moved to Ontario, so that's what I'll be talking about.

Your SIN

The social insurance number (SIN) is the Canadian equivalent of a Social Security Number or National Insurance Number. You will need this number in order to register for the provincial insurance plan, set up some types of bank accounts, access public benefits, and legally work in the country.

If you're lucky, you were able to get a SIN when you became a resident at the port of entry. However, if you drive across the border or weren't able to get it at the airport, then you can take care of it at any Service Canada location. You don't even need to fill out any forms, just bring your passport and visa to prove you're a legal resident. There are Service Canada locations all over and they're even open on weekends, so this is simple and quick.

The Canadian government does not issue you any sort of physical card. Instead, they'll print out a piece of paper for your reference, so make sure to write it down somewhere where you won't lose it.

Your PR card

If you've moved to Canada as a permanent resident, the government will automatically mail your new permanent resident card to the address that you listed on your CoPR document. This usually takes six weeks. The IRCC has a tool that estimates the current processing time.

Entering Canada without a PR card

Occasionally the news will feature stories of Canadian permanent residents who get stranded after a vacation, because they missed the memo that they need a valid PR card in order to re-enter the country.

Immediately after moving to Canada

If you need to leave the country before you receive your PR card, you probably don't need to worry. Bring your CoPR with you and be prepared to answer a few questions at the airport. Many people aren't able to wrap up their lives within six months, so the border agent you talk to won't find it unusual if you need to return to sell your home or take care of family matters.

However, this is at the discretion of the border agent. This unofficial policy of allowing new PRs to travel with a CoPR could change at any time and you may be required to obtain a permanent resident travel document (PRTD) to return to Canada.

After your first six months in Canada

It is very important to have a valid PR card if you leave Canada. You cannot re-enter the country by commercial plane, train, bus, or boat without one.

You can only renew your PR card from within Canada and you cannot have someone else pick up the card on your behalf. If you do not have a valid PR card when you want to return to Canada by commercial vehicle, you will need to obtain a permanent resident travel document (PRTD).

The only way to enter Canada without a valid PR card or PRTD is by private vehicle, because private vehicles have different identity document requirements.

Maintaining PR status

Letting your PR card expire does not mean you've lost your PR status. Maintaining your PR status requires that you spend every two out of five years, or 730 days out of 1825 days, physically in Canada. The time does not have to be continuous and is calculated on a rolling basis. You will need to submit a travel journal when you apply to renew your PR card.

Renewing or replacing your PR card

You should apply to renew your PR card six months before it expires. If you need to travel within that time frame, you can request an urgent renewal. Requesting a replacement for an expired, lost, or stolen PR card can be done online.

You can also request an updated PR card if you legally change your gender.

Your phone

Canada is known for having expensive phone plans. If you're moving to Canada, it makes sense to get a Canadian phone plan, but I've managed to avoid it.

Getting a Canadian phone plan

Getting a phone plan as a new resident can be a little tricky. You'll probably need to choose a Bring Your Own Phone (BYOP) plan, because choosing a plan that includes a phone requires a Canadian credit history. You'll need to make sure whatever phone you have (or purchase separately from a phone contract) will work with your new provider.

When choosing a plan, be careful to check the coverage area and roaming fees. Some plans are Canada-wide, while others may consider calls outside of your area code long distance and charge you extra.

Make sure you understand how much it will cost for you to call or text your home country (or wherever your friends and family are).

The Wireless Code of Canada provides you with certain rights, including the right to suspend service at no cost if your phone is stolen and to have your phone unlocked.

Pre-paid plans v. contracts

With a pre-paid phone plan there is no contract. Each month you pay in advance for your services. This is helpful, because it won't require a credit check. Some pre-paid plans offer a flat fee for monthly services, while others are pay-as-you-go based on your actual usage. You can buy a set amount of minutes, data, and SMS and simply pay for more when you're out.

A plan with a contract will likely require a Canadian credit history, a security deposit, or a co-signer. If you have friends in Canada already, consider joining their phone plan and splitting the cost.

If you have a contract, be careful if your plan is not unlimited. The cost of going over your allotted minutes, data, or SMS can be exorbitant. There are likely fees associated with ending your contract if you've had it for less than two years.

Life without a Canadian phone plan

The cheapest option is to not have any phone plan at all and use your phone on wifi only and make all of your calls over Skype or Google Hangouts.

If you're in a city where wifi is ubiquitous (and you're very stubborn and dedicated to saving money) this could work for you.

Keeping your foreign plan

Most countries have cheaper, better cell phone plans than Canada. If your phone plan will work in Canada without roaming charges, keep it!

Check the details of your plan, because some providers reserve the right to terminate your plan without warning if you don't connect to a tower in your home district within a certain amount of time, typically 180 days.

If you're coming from the US, you may opt to keep your T-mobile or Google Fi plan. Both provide excellent global coverage with no roaming and unlimited data.

Getting a Canadian VOIP number

It's helpful to have a Canadian phone number so people can call you without worrying about international charges. If your building intercom is connected to your phone, you'll need a local number for that. You can get a VOIP number through Fongo. Fongo is a little buggy, but it's the best option I've found so far.

Your new home

Finding an apartment before you arrive in Canada can be difficult. Border agents gave me the impression that it's common for the primary applicant to declare landing, get started at work, find a home, set it up, and then have their family join them before the arrival deadline.

Most people plan on staying in a hostel, hotel, or vacation rental for the first days or weeks they're in Canada if they don't have friends or family to stay with. Hostels in major Canadian cities frequently reach capacity for much of the summer, so you may need to book well in advance.

Another option for finding temporary housing before your arrival or immediately after is through a nonprofit serving newcomers.

Renting an apartment

Trying to secure an apartment when you're not there in person and looking in an unfamiliar market can make you vulnerable to scams. If you can't be there in person to find an apartment, working with a broker dramatically reduces the risk of getting scammed. A good real estate agent can help you pick out a great apartment, negotiate the price, and manage the paperwork. They can also save you the hassle of scheduling viewings.

Since the landlord pays the agent's commission, it costs you nothing. However, brokers typically don't bother with inexpensive properties, so if you're looking for a budget studio, you may be on your own.

A real estate agent or settlement organization may be able to help you find a home without the standard tenant requirements. Most landlords will want to see:

- proof of income
- your Canadian credit history (some landlords will consider foreign credit scores)
- a reference letter from a Canadian landlord

As a newcomer, you may not be able to provide any of these. Individual landlords (like someone renting out the basement apartment in their home or a single condo they own) are more likely to accept tenants who don't have standard paperwork.

You'll also likely need to fill out a rental application with information on who'll be living with you, any pets you have, previous landlord contact information, and employment information.

It can help to have your deposit ready. Moving money around accounts takes time, so make sure you can get a bank draft or certified cheque for first and last month's rent.

While it may be illegal for a landlord to require you to provide post-dated rent cheques or to pre-pay rent, offering to do so may be a way to get a landlord to accept you without proof of employment. If you do this, be sure to detail the agreement in writing.

In Toronto, apartment listings typically appear one or two months before they're actually available to move into. That's because landlords and tenants are required to give 60 days notice. Of course, if you need to move tomorrow, you'll be able to find places available immediately, but there won't be a lot to choose from.

Before you sign a lease, read it over carefully and check with the local laws. Ontario rentals use a standard lease. Most apartments don't include utilities, so you'll probably be responsible for hydro (electric), water, and internet/cable/phone. Be sure you understand what's included in your rent and what's not.

Most leases are for 12 months and automatically become month-to-month afterward. If you're on a month-to-month lease, tenants are required to give 60 days notice before moving out.

Laws governing housing vary from place to place, so check with your province and municipality for local regulations.

Shared apartments

If you're having difficulty finding a landlord who will accept you without the proper paperwork or if you're worried about being able to afford rent in an expensive city while you get settled, you can find an apartment sublet or a room in a shared home.

Plenty of people have roommates in Canada to save on expenses. One of the potential downfalls is that co-tenancy means you're jointly responsible for the lease — if they don't pay, you'll be stuck paying. Technically, all tenants share the whole apartment.

Some landlords will allow each roommate to sign a separate lease. In this case, each tenant has a bedroom and access to the kitchen and bathroom are shared. This, however, may mean your apartment is technically a boarding house, falling under different laws.

In Ontario, if you share a kitchen or bathroom with your landlord, you are not covered by the Residential Tenancies Act that protects most tenants.

Buying a condo in Toronto

You hear it all the time: Toronto is way too expensive to buy anything! In fact, houses downtown are over a million dollars!

What's wrong with this statement? The idea that you need to live in a house right downtown. No one talks about buying houses in Manhattan or central London. Torontonians need to join their urban brethren and learn to live in condos, co-ops, and apartments like the rest of the world. Houses are for the rich and for the suburbs.

Luckily, Toronto has uncommonly nice real estate. Most condos are less than ten years old and boast luxurious amenities: concierge, fitness centers, party rooms, indoor and outdoor pools, saunas, billiard rooms, show kitchens, pet spas, roof decks, grill areas, coworking spaces, and gardens. Toronto's real estate is also significantly less expensive than other comparable cities.

What's a condo?

A condominium most commonly refers to a residential unit in a high-rise building, but plenty of condos don't fit that description. Condos can be commercial units, townhouses, triplexes converted to sale, or any number of other styles. You own the condo unit and share ownership of common elements, such as the building and grounds.

While condos are pretty similar all around Canada (and the US), the laws and terminology differ from place to place. You should always check with your local real estate attorney and real estate agent before making any important decisions.

The condo board

Condos are run by a board of directors, typically made up of owners in that building. All condo owners have certain rights, including the right to attend general meetings and vote on decisions. You'll get annual reports and updates about any changes. If the condo is sued, that includes everyone, including you.

The buying process

Early on in the buying process, I started dropping by all the condo centres we passed. There are a lot of them in Toronto. This is a great way to see your options, since you're presented with all the floor plans for building units. If you like the floor plans and amenities in one building, you can check out resale condos in other buildings by that developer.

In Ontario, you sign an agreement with a real estate agent when they start showing you properties, stating that they represent you as a buyer and will get a commission on any purchase you make for a certain timeframe. You don't pay the real estate agent, your seller does.

After buying and selling a co-op in Brooklyn, buying a condo seemed incredibly easy. I found a realtor, put in an offer, haggled a bit, and soon had a completed Agreement of Purchase and Sale (APS). I then provided a bank cheque for the deposit. The hardest part of the sale was getting the money transferred internationally.

Prior to closing, I wired the balance of the funds to my attorney's trust and signed some paperwork. Once all of the papers were filed and the funds were released to the seller, I went back to my attorney's office to pick up keys. And then I was done!

The data you need to buy

Your realtor can provide you with previous sales for your unit, building, or neighborhood. They can also provide you with information on how much a unit would rent for. Nothing is guaranteed, but this is important information to make such a big investment decision. Ontario's privacy laws restrict what information you can access without a realtor.

Have your real estate attorney review the condominium documents and status certificate. If you don't have access to these prior to putting in an offer, you can make your offer contingent on your lawyer's review.

Financing a condo purchase

The down-payment required can vary significantly, from 5% to 20%.

If you're buying with a mortgage, you'll want to get prequalified or preapproved before you start looking. This shows agents and sellers you're serious, as well as demonstrating how much money you can have access to. You are under no obligation to get a mortgage from the bank that provided the prequalification or preapproval. Remember to account for closing costs and the cost of moving.

As a new resident to Canada with a minimal credit history, it can be a challenge to get a mortgage. You may be able to find a mortgage through an international bank that will recognize your foreign credit history or use a bank that offers programs for newcomers.

Pre-approval for a mortgage is no guarantee that you'll qualify for a mortgage, especially when you buy pre-sale and have a months or years long gap between pre-approval and actually getting the mortgage. Unless your pre-sale contract has a financing contingency, you will be responsible for payment, even if your mortgage is denied.

If you buy a pre-construction condo, your mortgage interest rate may rise between when you make your offer and when your building is actually registered. You may be able to get your bank to guarantee the rate for much longer than normal for pre-construction purchases.

If the value of your condo at completion is less than the pre-construction price, your mortgage may not cover the complete cost you've agreed to in the contract. You'll need to find cash to cover the difference.

Maintenance fees

New construction is notorious for having artificially low maintenance fees to lure in buyers, which skyrocket during the first few years of ownership.

Older buildings may have higher maintenance fees because they're carefully budgeting for future repairs and upgrades to keep the building in great condition. They're also likely to include some of your utilities — that "high" fee may include your hydro and water costs.

Buildings with nice amenities will inevitably have higher maintenance costs, although large buildings can spread the costs of a pool over a larger number of units. The roof, elevators, and other utilities all require upkeep and upgrades over time. Buildings pay for snow removal, cleaning services, landscaping, security, and insurance costs.

A well-managed building will charge enough in maintenance to effectively pre-pay for large expenses over time, so costs can be taken out of the building's reserve funds. If the building doesn't have enough money to cover necessary repairs, the owners will have to split the costs by paying an assessment.

Property taxes

Property taxes are not included in maintenance fees unless you are buying a co-op or co-ownership unit.

In a resale unit, you can find out what owners paid last year and what the anticipated costs will be for this year.

In a new unit, you can find out the estimated property taxes.

Insurance

Your mortgage bank and your condo board will probably both require that you have insurance. Square One is one of the few insurance companies that will write policies for new residents without a credit history. They're also probably a lot more open to short term rentals than your condo board.

Setting up your home

Utilities

If you live in an apartment or condo, some or all of your utilities may be included in your rent or maintenance. This information should be in your lease or purchasing documents.

Each area has different utility companies. You can find all of your local utility providers in the Yellow Pages. You can also just ask the landlord, previous tenants, neighbors, realtor, or condo board for their recommendations.

You'll want to call the utility companies up to a month before you move in to create an account and schedule installation. Some utilities will charge you to set up an account and install service.

Some utility companies will want a previous address in Canada or a SIN. As a new resident, you may have to call around to find a service provider who will provide utilities to your home. If you don't have a Canadian credit history, they may require a security deposit. The security deposit should be returned to you, with interest, after a year of on-time payments or when you close the account.

Most utility companies bill you on a monthly basis. Some will bill you quarterly. Each bill is typically for the quantity you consumed in the previous month, although some utilities will have a flat fee paid in advance of service.

You can pay bills through the mail, on the company website, directly through your bank, automatic withdrawal, or over the phone. If bills aren't paid on time, you'll be charged a late fee. You'll usually have two weeks from when you get the bill to when the bill is due. You can have paper bills mailed to you or you can have electronic bills delivered.

If you can't afford to pay your utility bill, call the company and negotiate a payment plan, rather than simply not paying the bill. If you don't pay your bills, they can disconnect your service and charge you fees, in addition to the money you already owe, to reconnect service.

Internet & phone services

Many telecom companies offer bundled deals, consisting of multiple services, including home phone, cell phones, internet, and cable TV. Both cable and DSL internet services are available. The phone, cable, and internet lines are typically owned by the main providers, but they also rent the lines out to smaller providers. Each province has different regulations for the telecommunications market.

You can compare plans at canadianisp.ca or comparemyrates.ca. Generally it'll take a few days or weeks to get service installed and there will be a fee to do it. Companies regularly run promotions to waive install fees, provide a free modem, or offer low introductory rates. Make sure you understand the contract terms, introductory/regular rates, and cancellation fees. Any equipment provided will usually have to be returned.

Internet in Canada is billed based on how much you actually use. You can get plans for certain usage levels or unlimited service. Unless you chose an unlimited package, most companies will send you alerts when you're getting close to your maximum usage so you can either avoid the internet until the billing cycle ends or upgrade your plan. You can also choose between different internet speeds.

Depending on where you live, you'll probably be able to get service from Bell, Rogers, or a third party that uses the lines of Bell or Rogers. Some third party providers, such as TekSavvy, are cheaper and provide better customer service for literally the same product.

Canadian phone numbers have 10 digits — a 3 digit area code, followed by a 7 digit local number. Canada and the US share the 001+ country code.

Domestic long distance is 1+ the number. International long distance from Canada is 011+ country code + the number.

Insurance

Even if you don't own your home, it's important to have insurance. Like health insurance, it can feel like wasted money—until you need it. Some leases, condos, mortgages, and provinces require insurance.

If a guest falls and is injured in your home, you let the tub overflow and it damages your apartment and the neighbor's apartment, or someone steals your laptop, you'll want to have insurance to cover the costs.

Each insurance policy is different, so check the terms carefully before buying insurance. Be sure to notify your insurance company if you buy an expensive item, renovate your home, get a dog, or make other changes to your home that would impact your insurance policy.

Insurance policies can be paid annually or monthly. Make sure you're not getting charged interest on that monthly payment option. It's a good idea to review your policy and update it each year.

As a new resident, quite a few insurance companies wouldn't offer me coverage. Square One Insurance offers policies to new residents. They also offer flexible options, like covering people doing short term rentals.

What's covered

Insurance will be for either the actual cash value (ACV) of an item (which considers depreciation) or replacement value. If you have an old TV, ACV insurance will pay for what it was worth, which may be much less than the cost of buying a new version of the same TV.

Look over the policy and make sure it covers what you own—and doesn't charge you for coverage on things you don't. If your kitchen is ready to be torn out, don't pay for more coverage than you need. You can save money by increasing your deductible or opting for a plan that pays the ACV.

There are different levels of coverage. Basic coverage is known as fire coverage, since that's basically what it covers. Mid-range and top-of-the-line policies cover much more. Sewer backups and theft can be expensive without insurance, but some people are comfortable with that level of risk.

Electrical appliances in Canada need to be Canadian Standards Association (CSA) approved. Home insurance will typically not cover damage caused by appliances without CSA approval.

Insurance will only cover what you can prove you owned. I periodically take photos of everything in my home—including under the sink and inside my closets—to have a record of what's where and what condition it's in. I also keep photographs of receipts for expensive items. If you imported things from abroad, your B4 or BSF186 is a good record of everything you brought into Canada and its value. These photos and documents are a huge help if you have to file a claim.

Tenant insurance

If you rent your home, your landlord's insurance covers the apartment itself, but not your things. Tenant, or renter's, insurance will cover damage to your possessions, accidental damage you cause to the apartment, injury to visitors, and personal property that's stolen outside of your home.

Homeowners insurance

Home insurance typically covers damage to your personal possessions, injury to visitors, and accidental damage to others property. Don't insure more house than you own. Remember that when you bought your home, you paid for the land, too.

Condominium insurance

Condominium insurance covers damage to the interior structure of your unit, damage to your belongings, unit improvements, injury to visitors, and accidental damage to other units or the common areas. Anything that's not included in the standard unit will be covered by your personal insurance. The definition of the standard unit for your building will be in your purchase documents. The condo will have insurance for the building itself and common areas.

Furnishing your home

Canada isn't known for its excellent online shopping. I knew I wanted to buy a condo and furnish it so I could move in immediately, months before I shipped anything from my old apartment in Brooklyn. I didn't want to deal with the hassle of trying to find good deals on a million websites or coordinate pickups from Bunz and Kijiji. Which is how I ended up furnishing my entire apartment from IKEA.

There's a certain beauty to being able to buy furniture, mattresses, linens, kitchenware, and pretty much everything you need from a single store. I was able to look at items in the showroom in Brooklyn and place an order from one of the Toronto stores. If you're in a time crunch to get everything set up in a weekend, this is the way to go.

US stores like West Elm, CB2, Urban Outfitters, H&M and other stores sell furnishings and have stores in Canada. Their offerings are typically the same everywhere, so you can get an idea of what you want to buy without being in Canada.

Trying to order things online from international chains was kafka-esque. I tried to order a rug online from West Elm and eventually gave up after my support ticket was open for a month. They theoretically ship to Canada, but their online ordering system was down for weeks and they don't take international orders over the phone. Most stores are more open about not shipping to Canada, even if they have stores in Canada. Be prepared to pick up your purchases in person.

Canadian Tire is trying hard to fill the gap left by Target's departure from Canada. Their latest furniture lines are much more stylish. Home Sense is essentially the same as Home Goods. Walmart is self explanatory.

Your driver's license

If you want to drive in Canada, you'll need to get a new driver's license, but the rules depend on where you're living now and where you're moving from. In Ontario you can probably continue to use your current license for two months, but should apply for an Ontario license within 60 days of moving.

If you have a valid driver's license from Australia, Austria, Belgium, France, Germany, Ireland, Japan, Korea, Switzerland, Taiwan, the UK or the US, you are automatically granted some driving experience in Canada. You can simply exchange your driver's license. If you don't drive, the 60 day rule isn't super important, but you can't exchange your license after your current one expires.

If you can't exchange your license, don't worry, you probably don't have to start over. Check with your province to see what the process is for the country you're coming from.

US driving records

You only need to prove two years of driving history in order to be eligible for a full license. However, if you own a car you'll want to prove your entire history as a driver in order to keep your insurance rates low.

In order to get your full driving history you can request an official letter that outlines your history as a driver in that state. Most DMVs will have an option on their website where you can request your lifetime driving record for a small fee.

Your driving record must be in a sealed envelope mailed from the DMV. They will not accept printouts from a website or an envelope you have opened.

Exchanging your license

In Ontario, you go to your local DriveTest center to exchange your license. Bring your passport, visa document or PR card, and your current foreign license. If you happen to have any expired licenses you should bring those, too, as they may accept these as proof of the length of time that you've been driving.

If any of the names on your current or old licenses are different from your current legal name on your identity documents, make sure you also bring documentation to confirm the change of name (such as a marriage or divorce certificate).

You'll need to pass an eye test and pay a fee, and that's all there is to it. After dealing with DMVs in the US for so long, I expected this experience to be awful, but it was easy and quick.

Your money

When you arrive in Canada, your credit score starts at zero. It can be difficult to get a credit card – or even rent an apartment – without a credit history. Some institutions will consider your foreign credit score, especially if you're from the US, UK, or Australia, but things are much easier once you establish your credit history in Canada. You'll build your credit by getting a credit card, paying rent, and other things you'll probably do automatically as you get settled.

You don't need a credit score to open a chequing or savings account. You don't even need a Canadian address. I opened a bank account while I was in Toronto as a tourist and had no problem. It seemed like most of the staff at my bank in Toronto were also born in another country, so they were familiar with all sorts of scenarios faced by newcomers and temporary residents. You might have a different experience in a small city or a with less international bank.

Many Canadian banks offer special accounts, credit cards, and mortgages for new permanent residents. Generally you can enroll in these programs for the first two years after you become a permanent resident. This is important, because otherwise it can be very difficult to access credit without a credit history.

If you don't qualify for a newcomer credit card, you can build your credit with a secured credit card. This is when you put down a deposit with a bank and can charge up to that amount, in order to demonstrate your ability to keep up with monthly payments.

Most Canadian bank accounts have a small monthly fee, but it's easy to get these waived for at least a few months. Some banks will give you a free account if you have multiple products or keep a certain account balance.

Interac e-Transfer is how everyone pays everyone else north of the border. They allow you to send payments with someone's email or phone number, so they don't have to share their account information. It's not uncommon for your bank to charge a fee of a dollar or two to send them. If someone asks you to pay by email or text, this is what they're talking about.

When you open a bank account in Canada, your banker will probably be eager to get you to open an RRSP, RESP, and a TFSA. This is probably terrible advice, unless your banker is familiar with international tax scenarios. You aren't eligible for an RRSP until after you've filed taxes. If you're a US citizen or greencard holder, your TFSA and RESP won't necessarily be tax free. Before you get talked into opening anything beyond a chequing account, do your own research or talk to an accountant.

Do you need a Canadian bank account?

You don't necessarily need a Canadian bank account. If your foreign bank has low foreign ATM withdrawal fees and you have a debit or credit card that doesn't charge for foreign transactions, you could comfortably continue using your current bank for quite some time.

I opened an account with RBC before I moved up and it's been very useful for things like condo maintenance fees and property taxes. However, since my income is coming from the US and I have a no-fee US credit card, I continue to use my US bank account as my primary account.

If you're moving to Canada permanently or even just working in Canada, it's easiest to bite the bullet and set up a Canadian bank account. Just remember that if you close your foreign bank account, it may be difficult or impossible to open a new one after you've moved.

Ways to bring money into Canada

If you'd like to move all of your money in one go or travel a lot, you can simply withdraw large amounts of cash from your foreign bank and deposit it into a bank in Canada. Or change it into Canadian dollars or whatever you want to do with it. It's weird, but quite simple.

You need to declare this money at customs if it's over C$10k. They won't charge you a fee, but they may ask for documents to show that this is money you earned legally and you aren't using it to fund terrorists. Paperwork showing that the amount corresponds with cash withdrawn from your savings account, proof of income, or a letter from your bank will make sure you don't spend all day getting grilled by customs agents.

Bank cheques, US cheques, and money orders

Many Canadian banks will accept American cheques for a fee, ranging from $5 to $20. You can simply write a cheque from your US account to yourself at your Canadian account.

You can also request an international money order or bank cheque from your foreign bank, which you may have to do in person. This isn't the fastest way to transfer money, as foreign cheques take an extra long time to clear, usually from 10-21 business days.

Wire transfers

Wiring money from your foreign account to your Canadian account typically happens instantly. Unfortunately, some banks will require you to be at the branch in person to initiate this process, which means you have to do it from outside of Canada. Typically there is a fee for both sending and receiving wire transfers.

In addition to checking the wire transfer fees, check the exchange rate. If you're not getting the sort of exchange rate you'd like, there are a number of businesses besides traditional banks designed to get your money across borders. Some of them charge a fee for the transfer, while others build this into the exchange rate. Transferwise, XE, and OFX are popular.

US/Canada cross-border banking

If you're coming from the US, handing your credit card over is the fastest way to out yourself as a foreigner. The need to sign is outdated enough that many automatic checkout systems aren't designed to allow it.

There are a few differences in banking between the US and Canada to note.

- Accounts without fees are much more common in the US than Canada. Credit card rewards and the like tend to be less enticing.
- You will be asked for your client card number instead of your bank account number. Your client card number is your debit card number.
- US bank accounts are insured by the FDIC for $250k per account. The CDIC only covers C$100k.

If you spend a lot of time in both the US and Canada, it might be convenient for you to set up a cross-border account. While this is simple, it's probably not going to give you the best conversion rate.

Even if a Canadian bank has branches in the US, it's not actually the same bank. Banks in different countries are separate legal entities, so there's limited services provided by the Canadian counterparts in America or vice versa.

Royal Bank of Canada

A few years ago RBC bought the Bank of Georgia so they can provide online US bank accounts for their Canadian customers. This is primarily a system set up for Canadians to bank in the US, but it also works in reverse.

When I need to add funds to my Canadian RBC account, I transfer money into my RBC US account. Once it clears, I can then instantly transfer it to my linked RBC CAN account. I can also deposit cheques directly into RBC US using their app.

RBC US is an online bank, but it could replace your US bank.

- You can get a US credit card and US mortgage using your Canadian credit score.
- You can also use ATMs with your RBC US debit card.
- They don't charge you ATM fees and will reimburse you for fees on some accounts. You can use PNC Bank ATMs without a fee.

- There are a bunch of ways you can move money into your RBC US account.
- You don't need to use a fake US address to open an RBC US account.

Theoretically, I could get an RBC CAN credit card and they'd take my US credit score into account.

RBC's regular Canadian accounts will also accept US cheques without charging fees. To confuse things further, they also have Canadian US dollar accounts.

Many of RBC's ATMs will dispense American dollars. Their ATMs are a little dated compared to what I'm used to. The first time an RBC ATM failed to dispense cash because it was out of cash without displaying an error message, I panicked. Apparently that's normal here. Just like it's still normal to make ATM deposits using an envelope.

TD Bank

Once again, TD's cross border accounts are designed for Canadians banking in the US.

TD is the logical choice for cross border banking, since they have a ton of branches in both the US and Canada. However, they don't make it as easy as RBC does to transfer money between countries.

- You can move $2,500 a day between the US and CAN online or up to $100,000 a day over the phone using a wire transfer and they'll refund the fees.
- TD Bank will recognize your Canadian credit history in the US, so theoretically they may count it in the other direction.
- You can use ATMs in either country without any fees, but bank staff can only help with the account for whichever country you're in.
- They offer travel medical insurance while you're in the US.
- You don't need to use a fake US address to open or keep your TD US account.
- You do need a US address to have a TD bank US credit card.

Bank of Montreal

Like RBC, the Bank of Montreal has acquired a US bank in order to provide online banking for Canadian snowbirds. You can link your BMO and BMO Harris accounts online and easily transfer up to $25k in each transfer from Canada to the US. Each transfer takes up to two days to clear.

Transfers from the US to Canada have to be done via wire transfer and initiated in person. BMO Harris has over 600 branches in the US.

They make it easy to view accounts on both sides of the border in one place. They also offer a Canadian US dollar credit card.

Taxes & retirement planning for Americans

If you are a US citizen or greencard holder living in Canada, you need to file taxes in both countries every year. It's also to your benefit to understand the differences in the tax code so you can plan your future.

For detailed information on this, see my book Cross Border Taxes: A complete guide to filing taxes as an American in Canada. This book includes information on:

- Filing your taxes in Canada for the first time
  - dealing with currency conversions
  - filing when you're missing documents
  - ending your state tax obligations
- Understanding the tax treaty
  - Foreign earned income exclusion
  - Foreign housing exclusion
  - other tax credits and deductions for expats and immigrants
  - when your spouse is not a US tax resident
  - when you have income in both countries
- How the tax code differs between the two countries in regards to:
  - real estate (personal and investment)
  - self employment
  - inheritances
  - disability income
- Filing your US taxes as a resident living outside the US
  - FBAR
  - FATCA
  - filing back taxes in the US
- Getting audited by the CRA and IRS
- Planning for your future
  - power of attorneys and living wills
  - tax-favored retirement plans
  - tax-favored accounts
  - social security and old age pensions
  - estate planning
  - retiring abroad
- Ending your dual tax obligations
  - relinquishing US citizenship
  - relinquishing your US greencard
  - the Canadian exit tax

Mortgages

As a newcomer, you have access to special mortgage deals at some banks for your first two to four years as a permanent resident. They'll either waive the requirement for a Canadian credit check or evaluate your foreign credit history.

If you have a job in Canada, down-payments are often only 5%. If your income is foreign (such as rental income from properties abroad or working remotely for a company outside of Canada) you'll have to put 35% down.

The mortgage application and approval process in Canada is much faster than in the US. It's unusual for it to take more than a week to get a final decision and you may get a decision in as little as a day.

Carefully check the terms of your mortgage before you agree to it, including fees, payment terms, overpayment and early payment options. You'll have the option to insure your mortgage in case of job loss or death.

Mortgage terms

Mortgages in Canada work differently than in the US. A 30-year mortgage in Canada needs to be renewed every 2-5 years, as if you are refinancing it at set intervals. This means that you could be denied a mortgage at renewal if your financial situation or the market changes. Your rate will change with each renewal, even if you have a fixed rate mortgage. This also gives you the opportunity to switch banks to get a better deal.

Breaking a mortgage

If you sell your home when your mortgage isn't up for renewal, this is referred to as 'breaking' your mortgage. Your bank will charge you a fee to do this and you may have to pay a portion of the interest you would have paid on the loan.

Your children

Public education is free in Canada for primary and secondary schools. The school year generally runs from September through June, with no school in the summer. School calendars are available far in advance, for ease of scheduling childcare. Education is overseen at the provincial and territorial level, but education is overall of a high caliber.

Classes take place from Monday to Friday. Most school days are shorter than the typical 9 to 5 working hours, so you will need to arrange for childcare before and after the school day. If your child will miss school, you need to inform the school so they know the child is safe.

Teachers are required to be licensed or certified. Children's grades are sent home in report cards, typically quarterly. Parents are expected to meet with a child's teacher to discuss the child's progress at designated parent-teacher conferences. You may also contact the teacher to meet with them if you have concerns to discuss.

Schools typically have a nurse, counselor, and settlement worker on staff. If your child needs additional support, they can help you locate it.

Schools are run by the locally elected school board. Most funding comes from the provincial and local level, which can lead to inequalities based on the wealth of a locality. Some provinces allocate funding per pupil, regardless of local funding levels.

Your children will likely attend a school based on the catchment area in which you live. In some circumstances, you may be able to request to 'cross-boundary' to enroll your child in a school outside the catchment zone. This is most common for students with special needs or in cases of shared custody. In areas undergoing rapid growth, like downtown Toronto, spaces may not be available in your neighborhood school.

Students with special needs are entitled to receive support, either in a regular school or in a school specifically for children with specific needs.

Transportation is provided by most schools, depending on the distance to school and the walkability of the area. Textbooks are provided, but school supplies are not.

School choice

You may be able to choose between school programs in English, French, or a mix of the two.

Some religious-based schools are publicly funded in Ontario, Quebec, Saskatchewan, Alberta, and Newfoundland and Labrador due to Section 93 of the Constitution Act, 1867. In Ontario this only includes Catholic schools. British Columbia has Sikh, Hindu, Christian, and Islamic schools. Students of any faith, or no faith, can attend these public schools.

Alberta has publicly funded charter schools.

In addition to publicly funded schools, which are free of cost, you can enroll your child in a private school or educate them at home. Home schooling is legal throughout Canada, but each province has its own regulations.

Enrolling your child in school

Contact your local board of education for enrollment instructions and forms. Some popular schools have waiting lists, so it's worth enrolling earlier rather than later to ensure your child gets a spot in your top choice.

Documents for school enrollment

Each school has its own enrollment requirements, but documents generally include:

- proof of age (passport or birth certificate)
- proof of residence (utility bill, lease, or bank statement)
- proof of immigration status (Confirmation of Permanent Residence (IMM 5292), Record of Landing (IMM 1000), PR card, Canadian birth certificate, or Canadian passport)
- information about your child's medical history, including immunizations
- proof of guardianship, if you are not the child's parent

Most schools require that students be immunized for polio, DTP (diphtheria, tetanus and whooping cough) and MMR (measles, mumps and rubella or German measles). A tuberculosis screening may also be required.

While schools may ask for proof of immigration status, all children aged 6-18 can attend school in Ontario, regardless of their immigration status or the immigration status of their parents.

Evaluating previous school records

Children enrolling in school in Canada are generally assigned to a grade based on their age if they are in primary school.

Secondary school students are placed in a grade based on an evaluation. This assessment is based on math and the language of instruction. Previous report cards, coursework, and other information will also be considered.

If your child needs support to learn English (or French), they will be placed in language classes. In Ontario they will be placed in at least one 'mainstream' class to help them interact with English-speaking classmates.

Your child's grade placement isn't final. They'll continue to be monitored as they adjust to their new school.

Canadian schools recognize the importance of retaining a child's native language, in addition to learning English and/or French.

Childcare

Paying for private childcare is very common in Canada. Daycare costs vary widely by location. Provinces typically provide a child care subsidy in addition to the federal Canada Child Tax Benefit and Universal Child Care Benefit.

Canada has licensed and unlicensed childcare. Unlicensed care is provided by babysitters, nannies, and unlicensed daycare.

Licensed childcare programs are overseen by the province, but not run by them. Staff are required to have a certain level of training and the childcare center is inspected. These include daycare, pre-schools, and out-of-school care.

Daycare

Daycare centers generally watch children from 18 months to the age at which children are required to enroll in school.

Family daycare is usually in someone's home and provides care for children of any age.

Unlicensed daycare programs are legal in some provinces, with restrictions on how many children can be watched simultaneously.

Pre-school

Pre-school is not provided for free like primary, intermediate, and secondary schooling.

Pre-school options include (in order of cost from least to most): non-profit co-operative schools, church-affiliated schools, local community schools, and private schools. Church schools do not require that children be of the same faith as the school and the amount of religious instruction varies widely.

Out-of-school care

Out-of-school care provides childcare before and after the school day. They also provide care during school holidays.

Summer camps

Many parents send their children to summer camps while school is not in session. Camps may be during the day, like school, or sleep-away camps, where children stay at the camp for a week or even the entire summer. Camps may have academic, athletic, or religious themes. The cost of summer camp programs vary widely.

Primary and intermediate school

Kindergarten typically begins at the age of five for children born before December 31st of the year of enrollment. In Nova Scotia, Ontario, Quebec, and the Northwest Territories kindergarten lasts two years (junior and senior kindergarten) and begins at the age of four.

The age at which education becomes compulsory varies between five and seven, depending on location.

Students in primary school generally have one teacher for all subjects. In intermediate or secondary school students switch to having different teachers for each subject.

Childrens work is graded throughout the year. They may be held back to repeat a year or moved forward, skipping a year.

Secondary school

It is not uncommon for secondary schools, especially those in large cities, to have an academic or vocational specialization. Secondary school students have a core curriculum that is required and the remaining credit hours are electives. Students receive career counseling and guidance regarding universities and other training opportunities.

Public education is compulsory until the age of 16 (or 18 in Manitoba, Ontario, and New Brunswick). Some exceptions to this are possible as young as 14, including for students who complete secondary school early.

In order to complete secondary school, students may need to earn a certain number of class credits, pass several tests, and complete community service hours.

Ontario offers students the option of a 13th year (or 12+). This is jokingly referred to as a 'victory lap.' While this has not been required since 2003, many students still opt to complete this optional year.

*In Quebec student attend high school until grade 11 and then attend a general or vocational college for two to three years, depending on the program.

Extracurricular activities

Sports are a big part of life at most Canadian schools. Training and practice happens outside of school hours. Most schools require a certain participants on sports teams maintain a certain grade point average.

Other common extracurricular activities include: band, choir, drama, the newspaper, the yearbook, language clubs, nature clubs, and student government.

Extracurricular activities are seen as being important to getting into university.

Your health coverage

Each province and territory has its own health insurance plan, but most require for you to wait three months after moving before you're eligible to access benefits. Regardless, there's no need to put off signing up, since it will take some time to process you into the system once you register.

Canada encourages you to sign up for private health insurance so that you're covered in the interim period before you're able to access the provincial insurance. You can also receive basic medical care at community health centers and pay out of pocket for services.

Stop by your local Service Canada location to sign up. Bring your passport, visa or PR card, and something that verifies your proof of residency.

Check which documents will count as proof of residency in your province or territory. A lot of the documents that validate your residency aren't readily available if you've just moved to the country. The easiest things to get your hands on are some sort of utility bill, bank statement, or driver's license. They may require that it be mailed to you and in an original envelope.

You'll get your health card a few days before you can start using it, which will be exactly three months from the date that you moved to the province. Or, if you apply after that three month window, it will be valid as soon as you receive it. You'll want to keep this in your wallet in case of emergencies.

Finding a doctor

You'll have to find a family doctor or general practitioner (GP) in Canada to act as your gateway to prescriptions and specialists. This is similar to many kinds of insurance plans in America, where plans require referrals from your primary care physician to access specialists.

You may have to look around to find a GP that is accepting new patients. One trick is to look for new practices that aren't already filled up with patients. Ask your coworkers or neighbors if they have a GP they like who might be accepting new patients.

Healthcare in Canada vs. the US

When I first started talking about moving to Canada I heard a lot of blanket statements from Americans about how disappointed I would be with socialized health insurance. In fact, I even heard that from Canadians. Americans seemed to think that healthcare in Canada would be more expensive and of a lower quality than I was used to receiving in America. Some Canadians would warn me that I would wait forever to see a doctor and would find that it provides less coverage than what I could get in America.

You might say I was skeptical from the start. My work puts me in the position of hearing healthcare horror stories from both countries, so I can confidently say that the worst case scenario is much better in Canada. How many people have experienced healthcare in both American and Canada?

Canadians may spend less on healthcare, but they still have a longer life expectancy than Americans.

If you have health insurance in the US provided by your employer, you've probably watched as the amount you paid for insurance went up each year. The annual deductible probably went up every year too, along with co-pays for doctor's visits, medical procedures, and medications. At one point, my annual deductible was 25% of my annual salary. When I moved to Canada, my job in the US didn't provide any health insurance at all. In the US it's very common for people to go several years without health insurance between aging out of their parent's coverage and getting a job with benefits. Even then, you'll see $300 or more deducted from each paycheque.

In the US, you are pretty much guaranteed to have a totally different health plan any time you start a new job. Or even a new plan every few years when you stay with the same job. This means changing your doctor and pharmacy and losing coverage for things like pregnancy for the first year.

In Canada I'd have health insurance coverage, no matter where I was working. I've found it much easier to get an appointment with a doctor, even with a specialist, in Toronto than in New York. People I know who've experienced serious injuries or illness in Canada are generally very happy with their care. It's the quasi-medical costs and loss of income from time off caused by debilitating chronic conditions that are an issue, since they're not covered by insurance. This problem is hardly unique to Canada.

What's covered

Your provincial health plan will cover most things so long as they are considered "medically necessary." For example, you can't count on the government to pay for cosmetic surgery. You can count on your health care plan covering physician visits, medically necessary surgeries and procedures, diagnostics, and preventive care.

Since you're not bound by a single health insurance plan with a provider network, you can go to any doctor in the province. That means no looking around for an in-network provider. You're also covered for emergency medical needs if you're travelling within Canada, and can see doctors in other provinces if you first clear it with your provincial plan.

Many people have supplemental coverage for things like prescriptions, vision, and dental. If you can't afford your prescriptions, your pharmacist or doctor may be able to help you.

Supplemental health coverage

Many employers will offer supplemental health coverage plans, which Canadians refer to simply as "insurance." Unlike health insurance in the US, you can't opt out of supplemental plans if they're made available to you. Your spouse and/or dependents must sign up for any supplemental plan offered through your employer. The only exception to this is if your spouse is already signed up for a supplemental plan through their employer.

Supplemental plans aren't universal, so they'll be different depending on what your employer offers. Most cover all or part of costs related to vision, dental, physiotherapy, pharmaceuticals, and travel insurance. You can generally count on a supplemental plan to help with whatever isn't covered by your provincial plan.

Most insurance plans will only cover the majority of costs of generic medications (for example, some cover 90% of the price and you're left to pay for just 10%). Often times you're on your own for brand names...sort of. There are some programs that will help pick up the difference between brand name and generic if your insurance plan won't cover the (often super high) cost of brand names.

Even when insurance plans fall through, there are still other things in place to help pick up the slack. Pharmaceutical programs differ by province and even by pharmacy, so ask your local pharmacy about what sort of options they have that might help.

Your new career

The idea of moving to another country without a job waiting for you is, well, terrifying. Canadian immigration programs require that you either have a job offer, money to support yourself, or a pledge of financial support from someone else. Plenty of people have come to Canada without jobs lined up and found their footing in their new country.

Getting a job in a different country can be incredibly challenging, especially if you require a LMIA. Even if you don't get a valid job offer before you arrive, these steps will help set you up to find a job once you're in Canada.

Economy & industry
- Three in four Canadians work in the service industry.
- International trade is a large part of the economy. Canada has free trade agreements with much of the globe.
- Canada is one of the global leaders in the software industry.
- Logging and oil are major industries.
- Canada is a major exporter of wheat and other grains.
- Canada's fishing industry is the 8th largest in the world.
- Film, television, and entertainment industries are growing.

- Tourism is increasing, with most visitors coming from the US.
- Toronto is the financial center of Canada.
- Jobs in Québec will often require French proficiency.
- Many companies provide bilingual services, so speaking French is an asset at work anywhere in the country.
- There is a large manufacturing sector in central Canada, led by the automobile and aircraft industries.

Jobs in Canada

In Canada it's rare to work for a single company for your entire career. The three most common types of employment are permanent employment, part-time employment, and freelance employment.

The most common type of job is permanent employment. This typically includes a base salary, supplemental insurance, a retirement plan, and any other perks that come along with your job, like paid time off. Generally, employment insurance, Canada Pension Plan contributions, income tax, union dues (if applicable), and the cost of supplemental insurance (if applicable) will be taken directly out of your paycheck. If you lose your job through no fault of your own, you'll be eligible for employment insurance payments.

Part-time employment works the same as permanent employment, although it's common to be paid hourly and not receive additional benefits.

You can also be a contract or freelance worker. This means you're paid a fixed amount (generally per hour or per project) with no additional benefits. Because income tax deductions are not made automatically, these must be paid at the end of the year. In some instances, you may qualify for employment insurance. Contributions to employment insurance and the Canada Pension Plan are optional. As a freelancer, you need to get a GST number from Revenue Canada.

Finding a job before you come

Finding a job in Canada before you arrive can be difficult, especially if you require a work permit. However, it's not impossible. Your chances differ dramatically depending on your industry, experience, and personal connections. Arranging for a work permit adds a layer of expense and complexity for employers. Even if you don't require a work permit, employers may prefer local candidates who they can meet with multiple times before making a hiring decision.

One of the best ways to find a job in Canada before you actually move is to apply to jobs from abroad and schedule interviews during visits to Canada. Obviously, this may not be realistic for your situation. If you have friends in

Canada, list their address on your resume, or simply list the city you'll be moving to. You can get a VOIP number so you can list a local phone number and have it ring to your cell phone anywhere in the world.

Finding a job requires a multi-pronged approach. Use your personal network, apply to job postings, and reach out to companies you're particularly interested in. While you shouldn't expect an employment agency to find you a job, it's still helpful to register with them and follow up to keep yourself at top of mind. Many cities have job fairs, where you can meet hiring managers, practice your interview skills, and see what sort of skills are in demand.

Don't overwhelm and discourage yourself by applying to 50 jobs in one day. Aim to spend a few hours each week sending out actual applications, but make sure to get out to meet your new neighbors and rebuild your professional network.

Finding a job through the Express Entry Job Bank

If you're applying to become a permanent resident through Express Entry, you have access to Job Match. You can't register with the Job Match until you create your Express Entry profile.

Once you create your Express Entry profile, you'll get a message saying your profile is accepted and directing you to the Job Bank. The message will contain a PDF with your Job Bank Validation Code. You need this code to create your Job Match account.

Job Match will connect potential employees with companies that have job openings with LMIAs. After going through the regular interview process, employers will provide candidates with information to include in their Express Entry profile. This will award you an additional CRS points and you'll almost certainly get an Invitation to Apply.

Getting your credentials recognized

Unfortunately, qualifying for permanent resident status in Canada or an open work permit is not a guarantee that your credentials will be recognized by employers.

If you are in a field that requires licensing or certification, you will need to contact the licensing organization to find out what requirements there are to get your credentials recognized. You should start this process before you immigrate to Canada. In fact, it's a good idea to see what the requirements are before you decide to immigrate.

Bridging programs are designed to help people with international training get set up in their field in Canada. These programs are organized by your local immigrant-serving organization. You can also look into related jobs so you can get a job in your field while you wait to get your credentials assessed or get re-licensed in Canada.

Networking

Many job vacancies are never advertised. This hidden job market consists of both jobs that haven't been posted yet and jobs that would be created if the right person comes along. In order to find out about these jobs, you need to know the right people.

Former coworkers, friends, family members, and acquaintances can be great sources for job leads. Hiring managers feel more comfortable interviewing candidates who come through a referral, since presumably you wouldn't have been referred if you weren't worth interviewing.

Even if you don't know anyone in Canada, your family, friends, and coworkers do. Let people know you're moving and will be looking for a job. Use your school alumni network. Use Facebook and LinkedIn to see who's in Canada who you can be introduced to. People you know who work for international companies may be able to get you in touch with Canadian hiring managers.

Once you're in Canada, or even if you're here to check things out before you move, get out and meet people. As you rebuild your social network, you'll inevitably meet people who will help you in your job search. Join professional organizations, social clubs, sports teams, religious organizations, or whatever's interesting and relevant to you. Register with Meetup.com and go to professional events related to your career field. Volunteering is a great way to make connections and get used to life in Canada.

If there is a certain organization you'd like to work for, get connected. See if you know anyone who could make an introduction. Go to events where people from that company will be presenting and talk to them after the presentation or in a follow-up email. Interact with them on social media. Nothing is guaranteed, but if you've got your heart set on working for a certain company, it's worth trying.

Advertising yourself

Put yourself out there to find employers. Make sure you have:
- A profile on LinkedIn,
- A personal portfolio website, and
- Are active on social media

Finding job openings

Many people find applying to job openings incredibly frustrating. Job postings often list off impossible qualifications or require creating an account and filling out dozens of fields. Some job postings will even ask that you complete a task before you've even come in for an interview.

While job listings don't have the success rate that personal introductions do, they're a necessary evil. Lots of people find jobs through job postings.

- The Job Bank aggregates general job postings from several sites around Canada
- Canada.ca lists federal public service jobs
- Charity Village lists nonprofit jobs
- LinkedIn lists jobs in all industries.
- Twitter can be used to search for job postings in your field and set up a list of companies and people you'd like to work for.
- Glassdoor lists jobs as well as reviews from current and previous employees so you can get an idea of what it's like to work for specific companies

Settlement.org maintains a more extensive list of job search sites. There are also many specialty job search sites.

Employment agencies & executive search firms

Recruiters provide employers with a short list of pre-screened candidates. If you make the short list of the most qualified candidates you'll move on to an interview with the company. Remember that recruiters work for the employer, not you.

Many employment firms specialize in a certain industry, which increases your odds that they'll have multiple openings you'd be a good fit for.

Immigration consultants

The skill level of immigration consultants can vary considerably. They may help you tap into a professional network and find a good job, or it might be a scam.

Volunteering

Volunteering while you look for a job can be a great experience. Direct benefits for your job search include:
- Getting Canadian work experience
- Re-building your professional network and make friends
- Getting someone who can serve as a reference for you
- Keeping your spirits up and keeping you busy during your search for work

You can find volunteer opportunities at Volunteer Canada, Charity Village, or by reaching out to a nonprofit that seems interesting to you.

Your resume and cover letter

If you've never written a Canadian style resume and cover letter, or just want someone to help you proofread it, your local immigrant services organization can offer you help. Your local library may also have services to help you with your resume and job hunt.

Writing a cover letter in Canada

Cover letters should be short and conversational. Write a generic cover letter and then customize it for each position you apply for. If you're applying for several types of positions, write a generic cover letter for each one. Be sure to have someone else proofread your resume and cover letter for you.

Address it to a specific person whenever possible. Be sure to include:

- What makes you uniquely qualified for this position
- Why you want to work for this company
- A reference to anyone you know in common, if you went to the same school or are from the same city, or any other connection to the company or hiring manager
- Your contact information

Canadian resumes

Resumes in Canada and the US are virtually indistinguishable.

You do not need to include your work permit or residency status on your resume. Employers may ask if you're legally authorized to work in Canada, but you don't need to offer up that information unless they ask.

- Use keywords from the job posting in your position descriptions
- Include any relevant volunteer work, especially if it was in Canada
- Include a summary of qualifications
- Quantify outcomes and achievements whenever possible
- Keep it to one page unless you're applying for an executive level position
- Include only relevant work history, or simply list the dates, job title, and company for unrelated work
- Use formatting to make it easy to skim
- Don't include a mission statement or "references available upon request"

The interview process

The recruiting process varies considerably from one company – or even one department – to another. There's no one set process that everyone follows. Be prepared for common interview questions and ask around to see what to expect.

Topics that are taboo in job interviews include citizenship, race or ethnicity, physical appearance, affiliations, marital/family status, disability, age, religion, and arrest record.

Phone interviews

When you have a phone interview scheduled, make sure you can be somewhere private and quiet at the appointed time.

- Look at the company website and social media accounts. Read any recent news coverage.
- Make notes with key points you want to make during the call.
- Have a copy of the job posting and your resume available for you to look at during the call.
- People find it helpful to stand and smile when they're on the phone.
- Take notes and always send a thank you email to follow-up afterward.

In-person interviews

It's not unusual for companies to ask you to come in for multiple rounds of interviews before making an offer.

Some interviews can last all day. When scheduling an interview, be sure to ask how long you should expect it to last and if there's anything you should bring.

- Research the company before you go. If you have the names of the interviewers ahead of time, find out their background and look for common ground.
- Find out the dress code. Look for photos of employees on their website or social media accounts. Ask people you know at the company or in the field. You want to dress one level above what you'd wear on a typical day in that position. Startups tend to have very casual dress, so you don't want to show up in a suit.
- Make sure you're on time. Aim to be in the area ahead of time so you have time to collect yourself and to not have to worry about transit delays.
- Arrive about 10-15 minutes ahead of time. Give yourself time for security procedures.
- Ask questions. Show you're interested and look for red flags about the company, team, and role.

- Follow up. A thank you note is a great way to stand out and reiterate important points – or add in something you forgot to say.

Individual hiring managers have strong opinions on following up and they vary widely. The best way to know what to expect for the timeline is to ask during the interview. If they tell you they'll get back to you in five days and you don't hear back, it's good to wait an extra day or so before following up.

If you don't get the offer, it's still a learning experience. If you felt you connected with an interviewer, go ahead and follow up to see how you could improve for next time. You may never hear back, but you may also get incredibly valuable feedback – or gain a mentor.

References

You can still use your references back home for a job in Canada. Be sure to let them know to expect a call or email. Brief them on what job you're applying for and anything you'd specifically appreciate they could mention in terms of your strengths.

You can use old bosses, coworkers, clients, and professors as professional references. One way to get local references is to volunteer in Canada during your job search.

Be sure to follow up with your references. Thank them for their help and let them know if you got the job.

Salary negotiation

Many hiring managers won't discuss salary until they're ready to make an offer. Many job postings will ask for your current salary or your expected salary. As a newcomer with a salary in a different currency and potentially a place with a very different cost of living, it's best to simply put your expected salary range.

When considering an offer, find out the details of the benefits package and consider things like what your supplemental health insurance will cover.

Employers who won't budge on base salary may be open to negotiating paid time off, paid training, business trips, bonuses, or other perks. Be sure these verbal agreements make it into your job contract.

Even if it seems like your dream job, don't sell yourself short. It's not going to be a dream job if you can't pay your bills or if you feel undervalued. Of course, sometimes it makes sense to accept a job knowing it's a choice you need to make to pay the bills while you look for something that's a better long-term fit.

Accepting an offer

When you get a verbal job offer, you don't have to give an answer right away. It's perfectly normal to spend a week or two negotiating details of the hiring contract, as well as getting some time to think about the offer. Thank them for the offer and find out when they need a final answer by. You'll also need to agree upon a proposed start date.

If the offer doesn't meet your needs or expectations, you can make a counter offer and negotiate the details of the contract. If you decide to turn the offer down, be polite. The world is a small place, so it's best to avoid insulting someone.

Be sure to see if there are any restrictions on what you can do after you work for the company. Post-employment restrictions and non-compete agreements are increasingly common. It's also important to read and understand the termination clause.

After you've accepted the offer, either verbally or via email, you'll need to sign the contract. Look it over carefully to make sure it includes all of the terms you agreed upon. If you have questions about benefits or details of the contract, you can ask to speak to a human resources representative.

Once you're satisfied with the contract, you'll need to sign it and return it. It's usually at this point that you'll fill out any required paperwork to begin your new job.

When you can't find work

It's not unheard of for newcomers to struggle to find work in Canada, even when they'd never had a hard time finding work before. Finding a job is very different when you don't have a strong network to rely on, especially when you're dealing with cultural differences.

It's not uncommon for newcomers to take 'survival jobs' for a few months or even years as they get settled in Canada. If you have PR status, you're free to work as a consultant or start your own business.

Working in Canada

Work culture in Canada is very similar to work culture in the US. Because Canada is so diverse, even if you feel at home in your Canadian office, you'll likely still be working with people adapting to a new office culture.

- Watch how coworkers respond to how close you are when standing or talking, as the distance between two people talking that feels right varies considerably between cultures.
- Avoid interrupting, pointing, or waving.

- Being on time is important. If you're running late, call or email to let people know.
- The ability to shift from teamwork to independent work is valued.
- Participation in group discussions and asking questions is important.
- Workplaces are casual but respectful. You'll likely be on a first-name basis with your executives.
- It's okay to say no to your boss, but do it politely and explain why.
- Avoid discussions of age, pay, religion, and politics when in the office.
- Sometimes it's normal for coworkers to become close friends outside of work, sometimes it's not.
- It's generally considered unethical to date a coworker, client, or customer.
- Talk to your supervisor about your career goals.
- Misunderstandings can often be resolved or alleviated by having a private, non-confrontational conversation.

Salaries in Canada vs. the US

I've heard a lot of conflicting information on what to expect of life in Canada in terms of salary and general cost of living. People in Toronto seem to think they'd make five times as much money in New York or San Francisco, but that is probably only true for a very small percentage of people. Rather than trust the anecdotes, I dove into the data.

Average salaries are about the same between Canada ($49,000 per year) and the US ($46,482 per year). Taxes are generally higher in Canada, but they're used to fund awesome social benefits like the single-payer healthcare system. That means that while your taxes will be higher, you pay very little for healthcare and won't see paycheck deductions for health insurance. At the end of the day, you'll take home about the same amount of pay in Canada as you did in the US.

The cost of living in Canada is less than the cost of living in America. This will vary depending on location and certain things will cost a lot more than you're used to paying for in the US, but in general you're pay less overall.

If you're moving from a large city like New York or San Francisco, you'll probably find that you'll pay less wherever you move to in Canada. On the other hand, if you were living in a small town or city and move to Toronto or Vancouver, you'll definitely notice everything costs more because large cities tend to be more expensive.

Are you a member of the middle class? If so, living in Canada means that you are now a part of the richest middle class in the world, a title held by middle-class Americans until 2014. Canada has a higher rate of social mobility than the US.

Canadians have seen wages increase faster than in the US, growing 22% since 2007. In the US, incomes have not been keeping up with inflation and economic growth, so people pay more each year but often earn the same as they the year before. On top of all that, the Canadian government has been more actively involved in the redistribution of income, preventing the kind of larger than life discrepancies found in the US.

At 331-to-1, the ratio of CEO-to-worker pay is double in the US as compared to any other country, Canada included. So, if you're a top executive, you'll probably make less in Canada than in the US. If this applies to you, you're probably not trying to immigrate to Canada anyway.

The federal minimum wage in the US is $7.25 per hour. For professions that receive tips, such as wait staff and bartenders, the minimum wage is just $2.13. The minimum wage goes all the way to $13.25 in DC and some individual cities have increased their minimum wage to $15 (San Francisco and New York).

Canada doesn't have a federal minimum wage. Instead each province/territory sets the minimum amounts, which range from $11.06 to $15 per hour. Some provinces have separate minimum wage amounts for people that receive tips, which range from $9.20 to $10.70 per hour. Some professions are further defined by special minimum rates per hour, day, week, or month. For example, a car salesperson in Alberta would make a minimum of $446 per week.

If you're coming from a city with a large job market, like New York, you may earn less when you move to Canada, but not a lot less. Different types of jobs might have higher or lower average salaries in Canada versus the US. You can use tools like payscale.com or glassdoor.ca to find out what sort of salaries you can expect to find in Canada for your profession.

Appendix

Sample work verification letters

To whom it may concern:

This letter serves to verify the employment of [your full legal name]. She is the [current job title] for [employer name]. She has been an employee since [hire date]. From [start date] until [end date] she served as [original job title]. On [start date] she was promoted to [current job title] and is presently employed in that role. Her current salary is [salary].

In her role as [original job title], she was responsible for: [original job description].

In her role as [current job title], she is responsible for: [current job description].

Please don't hesitate to contact me for further information.

Sincerely,

[signature]

[full name]
[job title]

To whom it may concern:

[Your full legal name] was employed by [employer legal name] from [hire date] to [last day of employment], in the capacity of [job title]. Her schedule entailed a 40 hour work week. Her annual gross compensation was [salary]. While an employee of [employer name] the firm provided life/AD&D, short-

and long-term disability benefits. The firm also covered the cost of her medical, vision, prescription, and dental benefits.

As a [job title], [your name] was responsible for: [job description].

Truly yours,

[signature]

[full name]
[job title]

To whom it may concern:

This letter is to confirm that [your full legal name] was a permanent, full-time employee with [employer name] as a [job title]. [Your name] worked at [employer name] from [hire date] until [termination date]. The terms of employment were:

Hours per week:
Starting salary:
Final salary:
Benefits:
Duties:
My business card is attached. Please contact me for any further information you may need.

Sincerely,

[signature]

[full name]
[title]

Escape Guide

Not everyone is going to be eligible to move to Canada. Perhaps you've simply decided life Canada isn't for you. There are plenty of other options to live abroad, permanently or as an expat.

Permanent Options

Most countries will allow family members to sponsor you for resident status. They'll typically have to show that they can support you for a certain amount of time and may need to meet other requirements. I'm going to assume that you, like me, don't have any family members who can sponsor you and aren't married to a foreign national.

Skilled Worker Programs

The Europe Economic Area

If you've worked temporarily within the European Economic Area (EEA), you may qualify for the Blue Card. This program allows temporary workers in any EEA country to work in any other EEA country, as well as eventually become permanent residents. There's also the Czech Green Card.

Australia

You can apply for a Skilled Migration Visa and become a permanent resident using Skill Select. You can apply for a Skilled Independent Visa, Skilled Nominated Visa, or Skilled Regional Visa.

If you meet the requirements for a Skilled Independent Visa, you can become a permanent resident without a job offer or family sponsorship. They also use a points system.

New Zealand

If you're under 55, you may qualify for New Zealand's Skilled Migrant Category. You can take this quiz to see if you're eligible or calculate your points yourself.

Countries to Retire to

Quite a few countries are happy to welcome you if you have a retirement fund, or even just Social Security income. This has long been a way for retirees to enjoy a higher standard of living for less money. Generally, retirees are given temporary visas and after renewing them a certain number of times you can apply for permanent resident status.

Some countries require people to be "retirement age" in order to qualify, but others don't. In countries with a lower cost of living than the US, the monthly income requirement can seem quite reasonable. If you have disability income, Social Security payments, a pension, an Armed Forces pension, or annuities, you can qualify. Sometimes rental income, income from businesses you own, stock market returns, or showing significant savings, and other passive income can qualify.

A few countries will allow people who are self-employed or work remotely to qualify for their retiree visa programs.

Countries that welcome retirees include:
- Argentina
- Belize – you or spouse must be 45+, can work remotely or be an entrepreneur
- Bulgaria
- Columbia – no age requirement, no criminal record check for 65+, may be difficult for non-government income sources
- Costa Rica
- Dominican Republic
- Ecuador
- Greece
- Ireland
- Malaysia
- Mexico
- Nicaragua
- Panama – 18+, no dual citizenship
- Portugal – no age requirement
- South Africa
- Spain

Entrepreneur & Investor visas

You may not think of yourself as someone who has enough money to qualify as a business investor, but many countries offer investment and entrepreneur visas that are within the grasp of many Americans.

Some investor visas don't require you run a company, they only ask that you invest in their country. Buying a nice house may be enough to get you a resident permit.

If you've always dreamed of owning your own business or simply want to buy your dream house, here are some options to consider:
- Columbia – $20k for businesses and $75k for property
- Dominican Republic – $200k for business

Temporary Options

Temporary Work Permit

The dream is always to get your company to transfer you to another office. This is fairly easy, especially because your employer's attorneys will take care of the details for you and hopefully provide a relocation consultant.

Nearly any country will give you a work permit if you have a job offer. Most countries require your potential employer to jump through hoops, like demonstrating that they tried to hire a local, showing you have unique skills, and paying fees.

You can also get self-employment visas, artist visas, research visas, and non-earning visas. If you're a remote worker, you may fall under different visa categories, depending on what country you're trying to get a visa for.

In Ireland, you can get a work permit for 2 years with a job offer, which is renewable indefinitely. After 5 years of residency you can apply for citizenship.

Freelance Visas

Berlin and Prague are famous for freelance visas. Remember, they're national programs, so there's no need to only settle in the most famous cities.

Your other options include Spain, Italy, Portugal, Dubai, and Japan.

The Italian freelance visa can be a challenge, but it's possible.

Work remotely

Working remotely on a tourist visa is a gray area for many countries. It's always wise to disclose to border control that your plan is to work remotely and ask if that's permitted.

Some countries are happy to give you resident permits if you can prove that you have a steady income. This is popular among retirees, but it's also perfect for people who work remotely.

Quite a few places won't specifically say that they offer residency permits for people with external income, but people have gotten residency permits without serious hurdles. These countries include:

- Argentina
- Greece
- Ireland
- Italy
- Portugal: The Non-Habitual Resident visa allows you to live in Portugal without working. It allows you to stay in the country for up to 10 years and can be renewed. You get special tax status.

- Spain: The non-lucrative visa prohibits you from undertaking any type of work or professional activity in Spain, but you are able to continue working remotely for an American employer and can perform freelance work for clients located outside of Spain. While each consulate might have slightly different requirements for the non-lucrative visa, there are numerous examples of Americans that have spoken to officials at their local Spanish consulate and were told that working remotely for their US employer is ok. Just be sure to be up front about your intention to work when applying for the visa to avoid any confusion.
- Switzerland: This is not listed as an option in official documents, but people have done it.
- Uruguay

Start a business

The Dutch American Friendship Treaty is a unique program to allow Americans to start a business in Holland with very minimal requirements. Here's how one freelancer got her DAFT visa and some FAQs.

If you decide to become a Dutch citizen, you'll have to renounce your US citizenship.

If you can get access to investment funds, you can get an Entrepreneur Visa in the UK. You can become an entrepreneur in Canada with a net worth of $250k (or more if you want to go to a popular province).

Teach English

You probably know someone who's taught English abroad. You may know someone who went to teach English for a year and never came back.

South Korea, China, Japan, Taiwan, and the UAE are known for providing lucrative teaching opportunities. Many include flights, health insurance, and housing.

You don't need a degree or a TEFL certificate to teach English abroad, although it certainly helps. Dave's ESL Cafe is the place to find out about how it works and find jobs.

Work as an Au Pair

An au pair is typically a young person (most often women) who takes care of children, cooks meals, and does some housework. Positions generally include room and board and a little bit of spending money.

Work Exchange

If you're over 18 and under 35, you can work abroad for 6 or more months. You'll generally need to show that you can support yourself while looking for a job and have your own health insurance. The visa fees are generally quite low and it's a lot cheaper than doing a study abroad program.

If you're looking for help arranging a work exchange and managing the paperwork, Bunac or Swap can set things up for you.

If you're interested in staying after your visa is up, you have the chance to build your professional network in hopes of getting an employer to sponsor you for a new visa. You may also find a new love interest who would like to keep you in the country.

Here's the scoop from a friend of mine who moved to New Zealand after doing multiple working holiday visas:

"Americans should apply directly through either the New Zealand or Australia immigration sites for working holiday. You can do it all on the application, no need for proof of funds or anything else. Each time I got approved in less than 24 hours. After my WHV expired in NZ I got a work visa through partnership with my boyfriend (family category), which is probably the easiest way to immigrate assuming you have an actual partner, opposite or same sex. You don't have to get married (same in Australia) and there's no real time limit on how long you've been together, but you should be living together." – Melissa B.

Australia

Australia recently expanded its work and holiday visa to include people up to the age of 35. You can stay for a year, but you can only work for 6 months for any one employer. Your significant other will have to get their own visa and you cannot bring any dependent children. US citizens can apply online.

Ireland

Ireland's Intern Work and Travel Pilot Programme allows US citizens to spend up to 12 months working in Ireland. You must either be a current full-time student or have graduated within the last year.

New Zealand

The New Zealand Working Holiday Visa is open to Americans 18-30 years old. It lasts for 12 months typically, or 18 months if you're working in agriculture or horticulture.

Singapore

The Singapore Work Holiday Programme is good for up to 6 months. You can apply for a new pass 12 months after your old pass expired. You need to be a student or recent graduate.

South Korea

You'll need to be a student or recent graduate in order to participate in the Working Holiday Program in Korea. You'll have to plan your trip, too, and provide a plan for where you'll be living and traveling. If you're 18-30, you can stay for up to 18 months.

Go to School Abroad

It's generally relatively simple to get a student visa to attend university abroad — and there are no age limits. The tricky part is going to be the financing.

Luckily, if you're American and looking to use FAFSA, they do fund some international universities. There are scholarships available, too. And, of course, some universities are free or very affordable. You can compare European schools for bachelors, masters and PhD programs. Many universities offer programs in English.

The best course of action is to contact the specific universities you're interested in, as they'll provide advice for obtaining a visa and financial assistance.

Many countries make it possible to get a work permit after graduation.

Don't like any of these options? Check *Just Landed* and *Getting Out* for information on additional countries and visa types.

Glossary

Acknowledgement of Receipt (AOR)
You get an AOR when the IRCC has decided your immigration application is complete.

Bridging Open Work Permit (BOWP)
If your work permit is going to expire while your PR application is under review, you can apply for a BOWP.

Canada Border Services Agency (CBSA)
The government agency responsible for immigration enforcement.

Canadian Language Benchmark (CLB)
This is the system for describing your language proficiency, on a scale from 1 (basic) to 12 (fluent). Your speaking, reading, writing, and listening are each evaluated and given a CLB.

Citizenship and Immigration Canada (CIC)
This is the former name of the IRCC.

Common Law Partner
Common law partners have a relationship that's similar to marriage in terms of commitment. To be considered common law partners, you need to maintain a common household for at least a year and, if you don't have a child together, have been together for at least two years.

Comprehensive Ranking System (CRS)
This is the points system for Express Entry. It's calculated based on your work experience, language ability, level of education, age, and adaptability.

Confirmation of Permanent Residence (CoPR)
Once you have your PR visa, you aren't actually a permanent resident yet. During your final immigration interview you sign a CoPR and become a permanent resident. Used to be called your record of landing.

Conjugal Partner
Conjugal partners are unable to marry legally or become common law partners due to factors outside of their control, like living in a country where divorce or homosexuality is illegal.

Dependent Child

A dependent child can be either biological or adopted. They have to be under 22 years old and can't be married nor in a common law relationship. Children who are 22 years and older but who are unable to support themselves because they suffer from a mental or physical condition are also considered dependents. These rules changed in 2017.

Draw

Selecting candidates from a pool of applicants. This is also known as an invitation round.

Dual Intent

If you show up at the border to get one type of visa while planning on applying for or being in the process of applying for another type of visa (or permanent residency), you have dual intent.

Educational Credential

An educational credential is any degree, diploma, apprenticeship, or trade credential.

Educational Credential Assessment (ECA)

An ECA determines if your foreign education credential is valid in Canada and, if so, what level of credential it's recognized as.

Electronic Travel Authorization (eTA)

People entering Canada who: are not Canadian permanent residents, citizens of the US or Canada, or come from a country that is not visa-exempt need to apply for an eTA before flying to Canada.

Excessive Demand

Your application can be denied based on excessive demand on the medical system. This is based on an illness or condition that would cost more than three times the average cost per person in Canada. This was updated in April 2018 to exclude certain common support services for people with intellectual disabilities as well as hearing and vision impairments.

Express Entry (EE)

Express Entry is the digital system of managing the Federal Skilled Worker Class, the Federal Skilled Trades Class, the Canadian Experience Class, and a portion of the Provincial Nominee Programs.

Express Entry Pool
Once you create an EE profile, you're placed in the candidate pool until you receive an ITA.

Express Entry Profile
The first step in EE is to create a profile, or expression of interest in becoming a permanent resident. This information is based on self-report and if you get an ITA you'll have to provide documents to verify your information.

Family Class
Citizens or permanent residents of Canada who are at least 18 years old can sponsor a spouse, conjugal or common law partner, dependent child, or other eligible relative to come to Canada through Family Class.

Immigration Consultants of Canada Regulatory Council (ICCRC)
The organization that regulates Immigration Consultants in Canada.

Immigration and Refugee Protection Act (IRPA)
The main statute pertaining to immigration law

Immigration Representative
An immigration representative has your permission to interact with IRCC on your behalf. These are typically immigration consultants or attorneys, but it may also be a family member or volunteer.

Immigration Medical Exam (IME)
Exactly what it sounds like, but maybe you didn't know the acronym. These are done by a panel physician.

Implied Status
In some cases your current visa is considered to remain valid while your application to extend your visa is considered.

Inadmissibility
If you're deemed inadmissible to Canada, you aren't allowed to enter the country. If a family member is inadmissible, it can complicate your application.

International Experience Canada (IEC)
Commonly known as the working holiday program.

Invitation to Apply (ITA)

Candidates who are chosen in a draw from the EE pool are issued an ITA. You then have 90 days to submit your complete application or your invitation will expire.

Job Bank

This is a job posting database inside of EE.

Labour Market Impact Assessment (LMIA)

A LMIA verifies that hiring a foreign worker won't have a negative impact on the Canadian labor market. This used to be called a Labour Market Opinion (LMO).

Lock-In Age

Once your application and fees have been received by the IRCC, you and your dependents ages are locked in and you're still eligible based on the age at the time the application is received.

National Occupational Classification (NOC)

Your NOC is a four digit number that describes the type of work you do. This is used to determine your eligibility for EE.

Non-Accompanying Family Members

Even if your family members don't come with you to Canada, they still need to be included on your application, since you're still expected to provide for them and could sponsor them in the future.

Open Work Permit

If you have an Open Work Permit you can take any job you'd like without needing a LMIA.

Panel Physician

Panel Physicians, formerly known as Designated Medical Practitioners, perform immigration medical examinations.

Permanent Resident

A permanent resident has the right to live, work, and study in Canada, receive most social benefits like health care, be protected under Canadian law and the Canadian Charter of Rights and Freedoms, and apply for Canadian citizenship. A permanent resident cannot vote, run for political office, or hold a job that requires a high-level security clearance. Permanent residency status can be taken away if a permanent resident does not live in Canada for two out of five years or is convicted of a serious crime.

Police certificate

A police certificate is a background check, detailing any criminal record, such as an arrest, warrant, and conviction for the person being investigated.

Some countries require a consent form before issuing a police certificate. If you need a police certificate from one of these countries, you submit the consent form to the IRCC in place of the police certificate and the IRCC will then request a police certificate from that country on your behalf.

Port of Entry (POE)

The CBSA facilities at land crossings, airports, and other border crossings. You need to go to a POE in order to land as an immigrant.

Provincial Nomination Program (PNP)

PNPs allow provinces and territories to choose immigrants they believe will help their economy. These programs may be part of EE, in which chase you'll be awarded 600 CRS points if you're nominated. If you're chosen, you're a provincial nominee.

Quebec Selection Certificate (CSQ)

If you plan on immigrating to Quebec, getting a CSQ is the first step in the process. This means Quebec has approved you.

Relationships of Convenience

A sham marriage.

Registered Canadian Immigration Consultant (RCIC)

This is the professional designation given to registered members of ICCRC. If you are paying someone to help you immigrate and they aren't registered with ICCRC (or an attorney), what they're doing is illegal.

Removal Order

This means you're being kicked out of Canada. There are three types. Listed in order of how much trouble you're in: departure order, exclusion order, and deportation order. You'll get one of these if you overstayed your visa, lied on your application, were convicted of a crime, or various other ill-advised things.

Settlement Funds

Money to support yourself and your family while you get settled in Canada. If you have a job lined up, you don't need to show proof of funds, but you probably should still have money saved for this.

This term sometimes refers to government funding providing newcomers with services.

Sponsor

A sponsor is a Canadian citizen or permanent resident who is willing to sponsor you to become a Canadian permanent resident.

Temporary Resident Permit (TRP)

Canada is a very reasonable country and if you're inadmissible, but have a really good reason to need to come, you can still get a TRP. If this applies to you, you want to talk to an attorney.

Temporary Resident Visa (TRV)

A TRV is a document giving you the right to visit, study, or work in Canada. It might allow you to enter the country multiple times or only once.

About the author

Cori Carl immigrated to Canada through Express Entry's Federal Skilled Worker Program in 2016. She writes about her immigration experience on WelcomeHomeOntario.ca.

Before moving to Toronto, she spent ten years in Brooklyn and grew up on the Jersey Shore. She is an avid traveler and history nerd who writes about her adventures in the sharing economy on RemoteSwap.club.

She works as a communications consultant for mission driven organizations and serves family and professional caregivers around the world as director of The Caregiver Space.

Cori has a BA in media and cultural studies from the New School University and an MA in communications from Baruch College, both in New York City.

Made in the USA
Monee, IL
16 January 2025

76863903R00105